Hints & Reminders

SHARON E. DLUGOSCH

BRIGHTON PUBLICATIONS, INC.

BRIGHTON PUBLICATIONS, INC.

Copyright © 1989 by Sharon E. Dlugosch

Brighton Publications, Inc.
P.O. Box 12706
New Brighton, MN 55112
(612)636-2220

First Edition: 1989
Reprint: 1995

Library of Congress Cataloging-in-Publication Data

Dlugosch, Sharon.
    Wedding hints & reminders

    Includes index.

    1. Wedding etiquette. I. Title. II. Title: Wedding hints and reminders
    BJ2051.D58 1989
    395'.22—dc20   89-9741

ISBN 0-918420-09-1

Printed in the United States of America

Acknowledgement

Many thanks to the gracious experts for their help in making much of the information in this book available.

Jean Andersen - Marketing Manager, Social Division,
        Taylor Corporation
Joan Bakken - Bridal Consultant, Minnesota Fabrics
Jennifer Deters - Catering Manager
Gayle Knight - Travel Consultant
Moya McGinn Conway - Director of Liturgy & Music
Virginia Sande - Flower Consultant
Anitah Sazama - Color Consultant,
        The Sazama Institute of Color
Arlene Sowden - Seamstress
Nancy Tate - Home Economist, Minnesota Fabrics

Contents

Introduction

This book was written to help you with the many planning details that are a part of your wedding. For some of you, planning a wedding may not be intimidating, because you've had the benefit of a friend's or sister's experience. For others, this may be the first time you've had to plan a big event. For all of you, these hints and reminders will see you through the questions and dilemmas that are always a part of every wedding.

These useful hints and reminders will save you time, money, and perhaps embarrassment. They are assembled from the collective wisdom of experts and the real-life experiences of newlyweds and their parents. This collection of hints and reminders is organized into convenient categories. Each category covers a different part of wedding planning. For that reason, any hint or reminder is easy to find when you need a quick reference.

The categories deal with every aspect of planning a wedding, from invitations to thank-you notes. Ceremony and reception planning is covered in great detail. Every wedding concern, including obtaining the marriage license, accommodating out-of-town guests, and planning the honeymoon, is given attention. In addition, there are suggestions for a variety of pre-wedding parties.

Each hint and reminder is given to help you plan a wonderful and memorable wedding. Do what is reasonably possible and then relax.

Enjoy your wedding day!

1.
Wedding
Plans

Start planning.

☐ Draw up a list of wedding activities and traditions that you think should be a part of your wedding. At the same time, estimate the number of guests you expect to attend the wedding.

Dollars available.

☐ Add up the dollar amount you can contribute to your wedding, plus any other contributions, such as the groom's parents hosting the rehearsal dinner.

Allocate funds to each budget area.

☐ Divide all expenses into categories, and decide how much to spend in each category. If your wedding dress is more important to you than the wedding photos, then allot more of your budget to the dress category.

Keep the budget handy.

☐ Once you have resolved any problems in your budget, put the final budget on paper and place it in a clear plastic protector. Always refer to the budget before making any financial commitment.

Receipts and contracts.

☐ Keep the budget in a folder that has pockets. Add business-size envelopes, enough so there is an envelope for each wedding category. Label each envelope and put receipts and any contracts in the appropriate envelope. Jot down the expenses and total on the outside of the envelope after each purchase.

Determine the size of the guest list.

☐ Request a final guest list from both sets of parents as soon as possible.

☐ Consult your budget categories to see if the number of guests you are contemplating is going to put you over budget. If so, you have three options: (1)Cut the guest list;

(2)decrease the budget in other areas such as flowers, wedding attire, or photography; or (3)increase the amount you are willing to spend on your wedding.

Index card system.

☐ Most people use index cards to keep track of guests. This is how it works: On each card, write down the name of a guest (last name first), address, and type of invitation mailed (invitations to ceremony, reception, or both). Arrange the cards in alphabetical order and place them in a cardboard box, metal file box, or even a narrow shoe box.

Looseleaf notebook system.

☐ Find a small looseleaf notebook with alphabetical dividers to keep track of your guest list. Assign one page to each guest invited. Record the name (last name first), address, and type of invitation mailed.

Computer system.

☐ If you have access to a computer, record your guest list on a database or spreadsheet software package. Enter the information into the computor and simply call up any information you need on the screen. Printouts can be made at any time.

Put additional information in the guest list system.

☐ Besides the basic name and address information, add space for the R.S.V.P., the kind of gift received from a shower or the wedding, and the date the thank-you note was sent.

Keep wedding attendant details straight.

☐ Draw columns for each attendant to show their wedding clothes size and, if necessary, their shoe size.

☐ Add a column if bridesmaids' headpieces need to be fitted.

☐ Add another column for the appropriate attendant floral

bouquets and boutonnieres. List the kind and when they will be delivered or picked up.

☐ If an attendant is coming from out of town, add a column for accommodations and any transportation needed.

☐ Reserve space for naming the thank-you gifts you plan to give to your attendants. Check off the spaces when you have the gifts in hand.

Purchase calendars for the attendants.

☐ Shop for decorative calendars appropriate for each attendant and mark important wedding dates in red. Remember to mark the dates for shopping trips, fitting appointments, showers, pre-wedding parties, and any pre-wedding photography sessions and rehearsals.

Use a master calendar.

☐ Make a list of everything that has to be done before the wedding and assign a date on the calendar for the deadline of each task. Try to stagger the tasks so there is never too much to do in any given week.

☐ Give yourself a wedding present: Plan to do only absolute necessities the final week before your wedding.

☐ Double-check any dates for appointments with wedding planners or attendants and any dates for pre-wedding socializing, and mark these on your calendar, as well.

☐ If your mother is closely involved in your wedding, she will appreciate a copy of this master calendar, too. Be very careful though, to update her calendar as soon as anything changes.

☐ Transfer the information on your calendar to your date book so you have correct information with you at all times.

Wedding service information.

☐ On a sheet of paper, write the kind of wedding service, (photographer or florist, for instance), the business name, the address, and the telephone number.

▣ Put down any details of the service supplied, the date, the time, the cost, and anything else that is necessary when dealing with each particular service.

Comparing services.

☐ If you are comparing floral shops, for instance, on a separate sheet make columns for their name, the kinds of arrangements, the service and expertise they can supply, and the expense. Then, at a glance, you'll have the necessary information to make a decision.

Prepare a list of what you need from each service.

▣ Prepare a list of things you require from each service. For example, prepare a list of "must-have photos" for your photographer. Or, compile a list of songs that you want the band to play at the reception.

List any information that a wedding service may require.

▣ List on paper any information a service may need. For example, a florist will need the address of the site to deliver the flowers, as well as the date and time of day. The florist will also need the name of a person to contact at the delivery site and the person's telephone number.

File the information.

☐ Collect the written information for each service and put it in a labeled folder with pockets. Any time you have a question about photography, flowers, or anything else, turn to the appropriate folder.

List wedding tasks.

▣ On separate sheets of paper, write the name of one category of wedding task, with columns of space for each task. Write the name of the person responsible for the task and make a check mark when the task is complete. The list for the ceremony category could include location, officiant, flowers, huppah, pew decorations, aisle carpet or runner, cushion for ring bearer, soloist and accompanist, and flowers for the wedding party.

List any special equipment or electrical outlets needed.

☐ Your soloist may need a microphone, or your catering group may need special hook-ups or additional electrical hook-ups

List special space requirements.

☐ You may need more space to set up an extra dance floor, or you may require a safe place to put gifts that are brought to the reception.

Note how much time a service will require of you on the wedding day.

☞ The main time requirement on your wedding day is the time you spend posing for the wedding photos. You'll also have to set a certain amount of time for receiving the wedding cake, the flower arrangements, and so on. It's best if someone else can handle these important details.

List any announcements needed during the wedding.

☐ An announcement may be needed to tell guests to enter the dining area. If there is a dance, you'll need an announcement for the first wedding dance.

Prepare a "thoughtfulness" list for out-of-town guests.

☑ List out-of-town guests who will need transportation from the airport, train, or bus station, who will act as chauffeur, the date, and the time.

☐ Make a list of guests who will need overnight accommodations.

☐ List guests who will arrive the day before the wedding and would appreciate an activity or get-together arranged for them.

☐ Make a list for those guests who would appreciate knowing the city highlights, public zoos, art galleries, and fine restaurants.

Prepare a list of guests' special needs.

☐ Compile a list for the caterer listing any guests who are on a special diet.

☐ Make a list of any guests who will need special access to the ceremony or reception and any special facilities they require.

Keep your plans and information together.

☐ If you use folders or index cards in boxes, find a very sturdy cardboard box to keep everything together.

☐ If your guest list is in a looseleaf notebook, put the notebook and your other folders into an expanding folder. Use the kind that has sections with a fabric ribbon so you can tie it shut securely.

☑ If you are using a computer, file every piece of information in the computer so you can bring it up on the screen for viewing or printing.

2.
Invitations

The right timing.

☐ Order your invitations six to eight weeks *before the date the invitations are scheduled to be mailed.* Some caterers need a final guest count more than a week before the wedding.

Weigh it well.

☐ To be sure you have the correct postage, collect a sample of the invitations, envelope, and anything else you want to go in the package. Then, take the package to the post office and have it weighed for the correct postage amount.

Postage costs.

☐ You can cut postage costs by choosing a lightweight paper, cutting down on the number of enclosures, or omitting the second envelope containing the invitation.

Postcard invitations.

☐ If you're planning an informal wedding, send postcard invitations instead of the traditional invitation and envelope.

Assuring response!

☐ If you think your family and friends will respond with a simple R.S.V.P. at the bottom of the invitation, fine. Otherwise, enclose a printed R.S.V.P. card along with a stamped, self-addressed envelope. Response cards and envelopes are worth the added cost. You can make up the printing cost by saving yourself approximately the cost of a ten-dollar-a-plate dinner for four guests.

Postcard responses.

☐ Postcards are sometimes used as response enclosures. Although this practice is not considered socially acceptable everywhere, it does cut down on postage costs.

Telephone answering services.

☐ Some brides make it even easier for their guests to

respond by enlisting the help of a telephone answering service. The guests simply call in their R.S.V.P.s.

Better safe than sorry.

☐ Be sure to confirm the time, place, and date of the ceremony before you give your final approval of the invitations. The same rule applies to the reception.

Check everything before printing.

☐ Read everything carefully before giving your permission for printing. Check over dates and the spelling of names carefully. Sometimes *Brian* will be spelled as *Bryan*, or *Catherine* instead of *Katherine*.

Oops!

☐ Order extra envelopes in case of addressing mistakes. Order extras of invitations, enclosures, and so on, for safety's sake.

The art of handwriting.

☐ Consider handwritten, rather than printed, invitations if your guest list is small. Handwritten invitations are accepted as proper etiquette.

A calligrapher's style.

☐ A calligrapher can create unique lettering styles, even artwork, for your invitations.

☐ Though your invitations may be printed, a calligrapher can write the addresses to match the printing style.

Legible handwriting.

☐ If your handwriting leaves something to be desired, ask someone with a legible hand to address your invitations for you.

Match the invitation to the kind of ceremony.

☐ The choice of phrasing in your invitation depends on what

type of ceremony will be held. Choose "the honour of your company" for a religious ceremony and "the pleasure of your company" for a civil ceremony.

The wedding hosts' names.

☐ Most invitations begin with the wedding hosts' names, usually the bride's parents.

Divorced parents.

☐ Usually the parent who raised the daughter is mentioned as host of the wedding.

☐ Divorced parents can simply list their first and last names, instead of "Mr." and "Mrs."

Names and numbers.

☐ Spell out all names and numbers in the invitation.

Personalize the invitation.

☐ You can add a border, drawing, or special verse to the invitation that represents the theme of your wedding.

Use color.

☐ A distinctive, readable colored ink and matching envelope liner will emphasize your wedding color theme.

Printing styles.

☐ The printing style can herald the wedding theme. Choose a flowing script for a sentimental theme, a modern type for a contemporary wedding, or a Roman-style print for a Victorian or Renaissance-flavored wedding.

Hear Ye, Hear Ye!

☐ Wedding announcements are sent to people who are not invited to the ceremony and wedding. Mail them close to the wedding day.

☐ Small "at-home" cards are often included with the announcements to let people know your new address and inform them of the name you intend to use after the wedding.

Organize yourself.

☐ A master sheet of every guest name and address, with correct spelling, will give you a good start in organization.

Use index cards.

☐ Fill out a small index card for each guest. Write their name and address at the top, and leave room to indicate an invitation sent. Alphabetize the cards. These same cards can be used to indicate the guest's response and record the gift sent by each guest.

Parts of the wedding invitation.

☐ Yes, there is a certain amount of tradition involved in assembling the invitation package. The invitation and a piece of tissue paper placed over the printed side of the invitation is inserted into a smaller, ungummed envelope. Response cards and envelopes, a list of events for the wedding weekend, optional maps, and at-home cards are placed into the smaller envelope, too. This envelope is then placed in the outer envelope so the front of the smaller envelope faces the flap of the larger envelope.

The tissue paper.

☐ The tissue paper tucked in with the invitation is simply a tradition from the days when the tissue was used to prevent the ink from smearing. It's not necessary today and you'll be socially correct if you skip the tissue paper.

Two envelopes.

☐ Two envelopes are often used in sending a wedding invitation, but one envelope is more practical and is acceptable.

Thermography or engraving.

☐ Most invitations today use thermography or engraving. Both processes give similar raised letters, but thermography is less expensive. Engraving can be identified by looking at the back of the paper. The lettering will be pushed up from the back and there will be an indentation for each letter.

Addressing the invitation.

☐ The outer envelope is usually hand addressed in black ink. The names and addresses are spelled out, not abbreviated. The return address should be in the upper left-hand corner.

☐ The inner envelope is addressed to the last name. If children under 18 are included, add their first name under their parents'.

☐ Don't include "family" in the address if you wish to exclude small children from the wedding.

Keepsake ideas.

☐ Send an invitation to yourself. A friend can drop the invitation in the post office on the day of your wedding so the date of your wedding will be postmarked on the envelope.

☐ Frame an invitation in a picture frame.

☐ Arrange the invitation in a wall-hanging memento box along with other tidbits from the wedding day.

☐ Decoupage the invitation on the side of a thick pillar candle to be used at subsequent anniversaries.

One final romantic touch.

☐ Purchase postage stamps that have an appropriate design, such as flowers or the word *LOVE*, for use on the invitation envelope.

Wedding
Ceremony
3.

Where to exchange vows.

☐ Most likely the church or synagogue you attend will be your choice to exchange vows.

☐ If you are not a member of a religious organization, you'll have to shop for a church or synagogue. Other alternatives are a park, a historical site, or a hotel.

☐ Your home can be a lovely solution, if the wedding will be small.

Make arrangements early.

☐ Any church, synagogue, or public place should be booked well ahead of time.

Think about the size of your guest list and the size of the site.

☐ When a limited number of people are attending your wedding, consider exchanging vows in the chapel instead of the sanctuary. If you don't have a choice, be sure everyone is grouped as close as possible to the officiant and the wedding couple.

The presiding minister, rabbi, or judge makes a difference.

☐ Practically speaking, if you find an officiant you can relate to, choose that person and forget about looking for the perfect site.

Meet with the officiant.

☐ Arrange a meeting as soon as possible with the minister, rabbi, or judge to work out the details of the ceremony. At the same time, find out if there are premarriage counseling requirements.

Premarital counseling.

☐ Premarital classes, weekend encounters, or questionnaires to be answered act as catalysts for discussions with your fiance about married life.

Counseling after marriage.

☐ It has been suggested that the couple find so-called sponsors, ideally a married couple, who can work on a one-to-one basis with the newlyweds before the wedding and even six months to a year after the marriage. In other words, individual counseling should be offered after the marriage, as well.

A private dressing room for the wedding party.

☑ Arrange for some area for your wedding party to prepare themselves before the wedding. Most churches and synagogues have private rooms where the wedding party can meet and get ready for the ceremony.

Greeting the guests before the ceremony.

☐ Traditionally, ushers are appointed to greet and escort the guests to their seats.

☐ Close friends or relatives of the wedding couple can also station themselves at the door of the church or synagogue to greet people.

☐ In some cases, the bride and groom themselves are ready and waiting to give a warm greeting. As one bride explained it, "This gives the impression of the celebration beginning with the ceremony rather than waiting for the reception."

Seating the guests.

☐ In the past and at most traditional weddings, guests are seated with the bride's relatives and friends on the left side, groom's on the right.

☐ If desired, rope or ribbon off one or two front pews on each side for the close family members of the wedding couple.

☐ Many couples choose an informal seating arrangement;

the guests simply sit wherever there is available seating. In this case, there is no "correct" side.

☐ Generally speaking, the ushers should fill up the front seats first to achieve a feeling of closeness and solidarity.

Ushers' duties.

☐ Ushers escort guests to their seat. They offer their right arm to the women guests, and the male companion follows behind. When the seating arrangement is traditional, the usher will ask if the guest is a friend of the bride or of the groom. The usher is expected to make polite conversation with each guest.

Preceremony time.

☑ Usually music is offered before the ceremony. This can be instrumental or vocal, live or taped.

☐ To help stir up a celebratory atmosphere, the song leader should encourage people to sing along. This presupposes that the songs are familiar and simple enough for everyone to join in singing.

☐ The song leader can also invite the guests to greet one another and encourage them to exchange names if they don't know one another.

The processional.

☑ The traditional processional has the flower girl and ring bearer leading, the bridesmaids following, and the bride with her father coming in last. The minister or rabbi, the groom, and the groom's attendants are waiting at the altar.

☐ This traditional pattern can be altered. As an example, the bridesmaids and their partners could walk down the aisle together, followed by the groom between his parents, and then the bride between her parents.

☐ One couple chose to have a liturgical dancer lead the procession, gently waving a pot of incense. She was followed by friends of the couple carrying Maypole-like banners and props for the altar. The minister, the attendants, and finally the couple, arm in arm, followed. The processional music chosen was one to which the guests could sing along. The guests sang only one line that was easily memorized; otherwise, they would have had to consult their programs and miss seeing the procession.

Recommended readings.

☞ Most often, scripture readings, old and new, are used for religious ceremonies. Ask the minister, rabbi, or liturgical director for recommended readings for weddings, so you don't have to go through the whole Bible looking for favorite passages.

Personalize the ceremony.

☐ You can include favorite poetry or choice pieces from literature, or you can write your own sentiments. Each church or synagogue has widely varied practices and restrictions. Consult someone who knows these restrictions first.

☐ Besides readings, a liturgical dance can be inserted in the program. One such wedding had the dancer offering a fresh daisy to each guest.

Marriage vows.

☐ The vows should be discussed with the presiding officiant. Each officiant varies in how strictly you must follow the formula.

Common language.

☐ You may be able to use everyday language that follows the prescribed form.

Important passages.

☐ Some officiants will simply point out the most important passages that should be emphasized, and let you express the sentiment in your own words.

The recessional.

☐ Traditionally, the newlyweds lead the wedding party out of the church or synagogue.

☐ The recessional can be led by candle or banner bearers, a liturgical dance, or anyone else you wish to lead the recessional.

Choice of music.

☐ Anything goes for music. Choose from religious, classical, popular, or folk songs. Remember that the minister or rabbi will have an opinion, and guidelines vary widely. Check first.

Music director.

☐ Talk to the music director. He or she can suggest music as well as available musicians.

Religious bookstores.

☐ Look in religious bookstores for music books and tapes.

Other weddings.

☐ If you've been to other weddings recently, use the selections that appealed to you.

Instruments.

☐ Choose the instrument you prefer. However, there may be restrictions on instruments as well as on music in some churches and synagogues.

Church choirs.

☐ If your church has a choir, you can make arrangements with the music director to have them sing at your wedding.

☐ The director and accompanist are given a stipend for their services.

Organist.

☐ You may have to use the church's organist rather than

asking someone else to play. Other churches will let you use the organist of your choice, but you still must give the church organist a stipend.

Finding an aisle runner.

☐ Some churches and synagogues have aisle runners on hand. Otherwise check rental agencies or your florist for a possible source.

Unrolling the aisle runner.

☑ The carpet is unrolled by two ushers after all the guests have been seated, but before the mothers are seated or before the procession begins.

When aisle runners aren't necessary.

☐ Many times, aisle runners aren't used, especially if the bride is wearing a short or tea-length gown.

Decoration for pews.

☒ Attach bows, greenery, flowers, or candles to the ends of the pews. Some places may have restrictions on the use of candles.

☐ Before deciding on what pew decorations to use, check the line of view when seated in a pew. If the flowers or candles are above the ends of the pews, it may be difficult for the seated guests to see the ceremony.

☐ Mark off the last pew you need for your guests with a standing rose or geranium tree. This is especially useful if you have a small number of guests in a large church or synagogue.

Flowers for the ceremony.

☐ Decorate the area with flower arrangements or potted plants.

☐ Check to see if there will be another wedding the same day. If there is, the wedding parties could split floral costs.

Props for the ceremony.

☐ Colorful cloths can drape the walls or hang suspended from the ceiling.

☐ Stands may be available to hold banners.

☐ Check antique stores for antique candelabra or Victorian prayer desks.

☐ Make your own kneeling cushions and use them later in your home as decorative cushions.

The church or synagogue may be seasonally decorated.

☐ When choosing the wedding date, keep in mind how the church will be seasonally decorated. For instance, on the days following Christmas, you can count on a profusion of green and flowering plants already decorating the church . . . and saving your budget.

Look at the decorations already in place.

☐ You may decide to take some things down temporarily. This is delicate ground, but you may be able to get permission to take down such things as schoolchildren's decorations or perhaps store an outdated liturgical banner. It's worth a try.

The out-of-doors ceremony.

☐ Line up potted trees, plants, pedestals, or columns to outline the ceremony's area.

☐ Fashion an arch of twigs, wood, or metal and festoon it with vines, and fresh or silk flowers.

☐ For evening, set up floor-based candelabra around the ceremony site.

☐ Provide seating for those who can't stand up for the length of the ceremony.

☐ Have an alternative site in case of bad weather. Reserve a nearby area to move to, or rent a tent with flaps so you can be protected from the elements.

4.
Wedding
Program

Wedding programs for guests.

☐ Wedding programs are usually an expected part of the ceremony, and they are often kept as keepsakes and mementos of the wedding.

Programs are useful.

☐ Programs allow the guests to follow each step of the ceremony as well as participate in the songs and responses.

Thank-yous.

☐ Programs offer an opportunity to say thank you publicly to everyone who helped in some way with the ceremony.

Share special sentiments.

☐ The program offers a chance for the wedding couple to share special sentiments with their guests.

Parts of the ceremony.

☐ List each part of the ceremony so the guests can follow the ceremony easily.

Names of participants.

☐ Include the names of family members, attendants, readers, musicians, ushers, minister or rabbi, anybody who is involved in the service, anyone who helped decorate the church or synagogue, or anyone who generally helped put the show together.

Time and place information.

☐ Print the date, time, and place of ceremony. This information should be featured prominently in the program.

Printed lyrics.

☐ Print the lyrics of songs if you want guests to join in the singing. If the lyrics are copyrighted, you must get permission from the copyright owner to reprint them. Write to the publisher and ask for permission to reprint. Mention your reason for reprinting.

Psalms or verses.

☐ Any psalm or verse that you feel conveys the sentiment of your wedding should be included in the program. In fact, a favorite verse could be used to decorate the cover of the program.

Absent family members.

☐ The program gives you the opportunity to mention any members of your family who could not attend the ceremony.

Motif or border.

☐ Design a motif or border for the cover of the program that represents the theme of your wedding. If you don't have a friend who is an artist, ask your printer to recommend someone who can do the design for you.

Program colors.

☐ Color coordinate the program to your wedding theme. Use two ink colors to print your program, or use colored paper and one ink color.

Cover verse.

☐ Type or pen an appropriate verse symbolizing your sentiments on the cover. Use calligraphy or a flowing script. Any printer can reproduce this if the script is clear and sharp.

Handpainting.

☐ Once the programs are printed, someone can handpaint a line drawing for the cover. This will be a big job if the guest list is very large.

Wedding portrait.

☞ Use your wedding portrait for the cover. Give the printer a good, focused black-and-white photograph to reproduce.

Size of your program.

☐ Most programs are 8 1/2 x 11-inch paper folded to a standard 5 1/2 x 8 1/2-inch booklet size.

Scroll roll-up.

☐ An alternative is to print the program on a 8 1/2 x 11-inch paper and roll it up scroll fashion. Tie it with a color-coordinated ribbon.

Framing the program.

☐ You can also print the program on one side of an 8 x 10-inch cover-weight paper. With an attractive border, it will be ready made for framing and hanging on the wall as a memento.

Do-it-yourself program.

☐ Type or print the information the way you want the final copy to appear, and paste everything on a piece of white paper. Add any designs or decorations. Take this to your local printer.

Freelance help.

☐ Hire a freelance designer to put your information into copy and take the material to the printer.

Computer help.

☐ Now, with desktop publishing, you can produce your programs on a computer. Once the program is the way you want it on the computer screen, you can print out the program with a laser printer and you'll be in business.

Give the programs to your guests.

☐ Ushers and greeters can hand out programs to your guests as they enter the church or synagogue.

Display the programs.

☐ Place the programs in a prominent spot in a wicker basket or silver tray and encourage each guest to pick up a program.

Extra copies of programs.

☐ Take extra programs to the reception for people who didn't receive one at the ceremony or lost their copy.

Printing quantity.

☐ Print more copies than the amount of guests you expect to have. Programs are often lost or damaged, and guests will want another one as a take-home memento.

Programs as mementos.

☐ Extra programs can be used for your wedding memory book or for keepsake craft projects.

Receiving
5.   Line

The purpose of a receiving line.

☐ The receiving line helps you make sure you're able to individually greet and welcome every guest to the wedding.

The receiving line at the church or synagogue.

☐ The receiving line can be set up in the entryway of the ceremony site. As the participants leave the ceremony, they can take their places in the receiving line.

The receiving line at the reception.

☐ Receiving lines are also held at the reception near the reception room entrance or to one side of the reception room. Wherever the receiving is, the guests should be able to move directly into the reception area from the line.

Personalize the receiving line.

☐ One wedding couple modified the receiving line idea. After the recessional, the two returned to the front of the church and greeted each guest in the aisle.

Offer refreshments.

☐ If the receiving line is held at the reception, ask servers to offer refreshments while the guests wait their turn.

Available seating.

☐ There should be some seating available for those guests who may be too tired to stand in a long line.

Members of the receiving line.

☐ This can vary, but usually included are the mother of the bride (if she is hosting the wedding), the father of the bride (but not always), the bride, the groom, the groom's parents (the father is not necessary), the bride's honor attendant, and the bridesmaids (optional), in that order.

A large reception.

☐ At a large reception keep the receiving line short—just the two of you, your mothers, and your honor attendant. This will shorten the time everyone spends in the receiving line.

Keep your comments brief.

☐ To keep things moving along, limit yourself to a few moments with each guest. Say hello to everyone by name. If you've forgotten someone's name, introduce yourself. Give a brief personal comment and if necessary, introduce the guest to the next person in line.

Bridal gloves.

☐ It is correct for the bride to leave her gloves on, if she wishes, while in the receiving line.

Decorate the receiving area.

☐ Highlight the receiving area with decorative pillars, large vases of flowers, a sunlit window, or a draped wall.

Adequate room.

☐ Be sure there will be plenty of room for the line to form and room for the guests waiting their turn to say hello. If the area begins to get congested, the ushers can redirect traffic.

Accessible reception area.

☐ The guests should have a clear path to the reception area. If the reception area is more than a few steps away, have people—either servers or friends—stationed to direct guests to the reception area.

Alternative idea.

☐ At a wedding where only the wedding couple were receiving the guests, the parents of the couple stood at intervals along the hallway, greeting the guests and giving them directions to the reception.

Reception
6.   Site

When to start looking for a reception site.

☐ Some couples plan their wedding for the date they can book the reception site. In large cities, bookings are made at least a year in advance.

Where to start looking for a reception site.

☐ Look at hotels, catering halls, clubs, restaurants, turn-of-the-century mansions, public gardens, and parks.

Amount of seating available.

☐ When you start checking for reception sites, find out the maximum seating space. Specify comfortable seating without being crowded.

Additional space.

☐ Check to see if the suggested area includes room for the head table, dance floor, buffet table, gift table, and everything else you may need for your reception.

Kinds of tables.

☐ Oblong, rectangular, and round tables are all used for seating large groups. Round tables are best for carrying on conversations.

Lighting.

☐ Check the lighting. Is there adequate lighting for the dinner tables, the cake table, and the dance floor?

Size of dance floor.

☐ Ask about the size of the dance floor. An adequately sized dance floor is about 20 x 24 feet.

Rental floor.

☐ If the dance floor space isn't large enough, you or the management of the reception site can rent dance board sections. Usually it's the responsibility of the rental agency to set up the dance floor.

Table appointments.

☐ Will the management of your reception area provide cloth tablecloths and napkins rather than paper; glassware rather than plastic ware?

Color choices.

☐ What colors can the reception-hall management provide for the tabletop linens?

Head table riser.

☐ Will the head table be on a riser. If so, the riser should be at least 10 inches high.

Riser steps.

☐ If the riser for the head table is 12 to 14 inches or more in height, a step up to the riser should be provided.

Table skirting.

☐ Will the management put skirting around the head table, cake table, and so on, and will the skirt be of fabric or paper?

Decorations.

☐ Who will be responsible for decorating the reception area. If you are doing the decorating, will the management allow you to tape crepe paper to the walls? Ask about any specific decorations you want to use.

Cake serving.

☐ Who will cut the cake—you or the management? If the management will supply someone, will there be an extra charge for this service?

Centerpieces.

☐ Who will provide the centerpieces and vases for flowers? Who will arrange fresh flowers in the vases?

Simultaneous parties.

☐ Ask about separate entrances, your own coat check, soundproof walls, and an area that can be closed to passersby if more than one party will be going on at the same time.

Wedding package.

☐ Ask about any available wedding packages. For instance, does wedding punch or champagne come with the meal?

Hall rental charge.

☐ Is there a charge for hall rental over and above the cost of the meal?

Tax and tips.

☐ When the price is quoted, ask if the total includes tax and tips.

Menu selection.

☐ Discuss the menu selection and the price range.

Food sampling.

☐ Ask if it is possible to sample the food. Take someone with you so you have the benefit of another opinion.

Guaranteed date.

☐ Always check on the guaranteed-date policy. Some wedding parties have been dumped for larger convention business. Sign a contract guaranteeing the date.

Overtime charges.

☐ Be clear about any overtime charges.

Guaranteed guest count.

☐ On the average, the reception host will pay for 8 to 10 percent more than the number of people that show up. Nine out of ten weddings have fewer guests than the guaranteed number. Keep in mind that if you go over the guaranteed number, the management will still feed your guests something comparable and not let them go hungry. Some services prepare for 5 percent over the guaranteed number, but ask about this; don't assume that everyone will be this forgiving.

A "maybe" guest.

☐ If any guests are "iffey" about coming, count them as *nos* on your final plate count.

Estimating the guest count.

☐ As a general rule, 20 to 30 percent of the full guest list will not attend the reception. Also, 10 percent of those who do respond with a *yes* to the invitation, won't be coming.

Check with unresponsive guests.

☐ Call any guests who haven't responded to your invitation. Don't be shy; you need to know how many people will be coming before you talk to your caterer or hotel manager.

Access to the reception site.

☐ Find out when you can have access to the room for decorating, cake delivery, and floral deliveries.

Cleanup.

☐ Will the management be responsible for cleanup, including your decorations? Some rental halls require you to clean up immediately after the reception.

Leftover food.

☐ Because of various health laws, many establishments will

not allow food left over in the kitchen to go home with the guests. This doesn't apply to the wedding cake. Check policies on leftover food with management.

The deposit.

☐ If a deposit on the rental hall is required, will it be automatically deducted from the bill, refunded after the reception, or held in case of damage or charges for extra cleaning?

Advantages of renting a hotel facility.

☐ Pleasant atmosphere.
☐ Room for a large number of guests.
☐ Adequate parking.
☐ Service oriented.
☐ Out-of-town guests can go directly to their rooms.
☐ Small children can be sent to a separate room with a baby-sitter.
☐ Dance space available.

Advantages of a hall.

☐ Less expensive than a hotel facility.
☐ Familiar surroundings, if it is your family's club hall.
☐ Choice of caterer (in most cases).
☐ Usually can be personally decorated to fit a special theme.
☐ Adequate parking.
☐ Special dates aren't as hard to obtain.
☐ Dancing space is available.

Advantages of a restaurant or club.

☐ Pleasant atmosphere.
☐ Service oriented.
☐ Adequate parking.
☐ Room does not have to be decorated except perhaps for the table centerpieces.

7.
Reception Know-How

Reception brunch.

☐ Brunch following morning wedding ceremonies is often a sit-down buffet or a seated meal. The menu includes breakfast and lunch items, with wedding cake served for dessert.

Reception luncheon.

☐ A luncheon is often less formal than a dinner. A picnic lunch can be served at outdoor weddings.

Reception cocktails and hors d'oeuvres.

☐ Cocktails and hors d'oeuvres are served less frequently since sit-down dinners became popular.

Reception stand-up buffet.

☐ Some couples choose a stand-up reception with several food stations, each featuring a different menu, often a variety of ethnic foods.

Reception sit-down buffet and dinner.

☐ The sit-down buffet and the seated dinner are the most popular meal styles.

Formal reception style.

☐ A formal reception speaks of crystal and silver, with elegant orchids, roses, and topiaries as decorations.

Informal reception style.

☐ An informal reception mixes glass and terra cotta pieces with lighthearted flowers, balloons, and ribbons.

Romantic reception style.

☐ The romantic country reception displays ruffles, lace, and bows, with fresh garden flowers in wicker baskets.

Contemporary reception style.

☐ The upbeat, contemporary reception boasts white freesias, calla lilies, or dendrobriums set off with mirrored squares sprinkled with rhinestones, glitter, and candlelight.

Coordinate color themes.

☐ Wedding party colors can be repeated in the linens and centerpieces for a pulled-together look.

Highlight heritage themes.

☐ Authentic recipes, grandmother's treasured tablecloth, and antique serving pieces highlight any heritage theme.

Display the flavor of your region.

☐ Allow the uniqueness of your region to come through with special menus, favors, or ambiance, thus heightening the flavor of a regional wedding.

Choose seasonal centerpieces.

☐ Seasonal centerpieces capture the time of year and make the most of in-season flowers.

Give some thought to your reception area before ordering centerpieces.

☐ Before creating or ordering centerpieces, consider the room dimensions, the ceiling height, and the table size.

Give special meaning to floral centerpieces.

☐ Include signature flowers from the bridal bouquet in each centerpiece.

☐ Highlight the centerpieces with red roses or the flower first given to you by your husband-to-be.

☐ Copy the centerpieces that were used by your parents at their wedding.

Additions to floral centerpieces.

☐ Balloons add a festive gaity to centerpieces, as well as extra height.

☐ Strings of pearls radiate a luminous charm, while rhinestones offer sparkle and glitter.

☐ A profusion of greenery, bows, and ribbon streamers enhances the small floral bouquet.

Centerpiece alternatives to flowers.

☐ Evergreens accented with bows and candles make a "scent-sational" centerpiece.

☐ Fruits and vegetables give an unexpected but lush look to the reception.

☐ Wreathes made of vines and accented with ribbon lend a whimsical air to the proceedings.

Centerpiece props.

☐ Straw hats decorated with flowers and tied with ribbons, or sombreros sheltering votive lights and strawflowers create imaginative centerpieces.

☐ Fans or parasols decorated with flowers and ribbons give a jaunty look to the tables.

☐ Colorful props such as Easter eggs, Fourth of July sparklers, Thanksgiving pumpkins, or glass Christmas tree balls provide a strong tie-in to major holidays.

☐ Seasonal props like kites, children's sand pails, autumn leaves, and pine cones remind everyone of the appropriate season.

Using candles.

☐ Candles are pretty and romantic, but only for after-five o'clock doings.

Placing candles on the table.

☐ Use candles as an accessory to the centerpiece, one on each side.

☐ Group candles in groups of three or five, each candle at a different height.

☐ Use candles singly, surrounded by a wreath or flower ring

Candleholders.

☐ Candles should always be placed in or on some kind of holder to protect the tabletop.

☐ Select candleholders to complement the wedding style.

☐ Use glass goblets, jars, small bowls, or compotes as decorative candleholders. Wrap these makeshift holders with ribbon, crepe paper, lace, tulle, or smilax and decorate them with fresh or silk flower blossoms.

☐ Ashtrays make perfect holders for pillar candles.

Purchasing candles.

☐ Look for long-lasting candles.

☐ If you buy candles in plastic wrap, make sure the candles aren't broken. Sometimes it's hard to tell, because the wrap keeps the candles from falling apart.

Linens, the underpinnings of the reception look.

☐ Color cue the reception with the choice of tablecloths and napkins. White tablecloths with color-coordinated napkins are the most popular choice, but pastels are coming on strong.

Renting linens.

☐ Try to rent floor-length tablecloths for a more finished look. Floor-length tablecloths are sometimes hard or impossible to find.

Tablecloth overskirts

☐ Trim the tablecloths with overskirts of lace, netting, tulle, or a contrasting color to give a fuller, decorative look.

Linen napkins.

☐ Linen napkins radiate charm and can be folded in may decorative ways, adding a creative touch to the table (See *Folding Table Napkins* for easy napkin-folding instructions. Write to Brighton Publications, Inc. P.O. Box 12706, New Brighton, MN 55112, for ordering information.)

Paper napkins

☐ Paper napkins printed with names or monograms are very popular. These can be purchased at the same time as the invitations.

Create wedding napkin rings.

☐ Add a touch of grace to the napkins with rings of green smilax and a few tiny flower blossoms.

☐ Paint tiny flowers in your wedding colors on homemade, white cardboard napkin rings.

Wedding favors, add interest to the table setting.

☐ Wrap Jordan almonds in tulle, netting or small decorative boxes colorkeyed to the table decor for your guests to take with them.

☐ Unusual favors, such as packets of flower seeds, candles, seashells, and paper fans promote conversation and are also very eye-appealing.

Chairs can benefit from a little fussing.

☐ Dress the chairs with a little imagination. Attach bows, ribbons, lace-backed posies, or balloons to the backs of the chairs.

Tables demanding attention.

Give extra attention to the head-table, cake table, and gift table. These tables should all have floor-length table skirts. Add ruffles, bows, ribbons, green roping, cord swags, or flower clusters to create a wedding fantasy setting.

8.
Catering

When to start looking for a caterer.

☐ As soon as you've decided on the date of your wedding, it's time to start searching for a caterer. In some of the larger cities, good caterers are booked a year ahead of time.

Where to look for a caterer.

☐ Sometimes the site of your reception—such as a catering hall, club, or hotel—provides a caterer.

☐ Look in your local wedding guides, newspaper sections, or the Yellow Pages of your phone directory for independent caterers.

Reassuring recommendations.

☐ Friends and relatives who have had experience with a caterer can give you the best recommendations.

Successful parties are good sources.

☐ Ask for names of caterers from people whose parties you have enjoyed.

Talk and compare.

☐ Schedule appointments with at least two or three caterers. Take notes so you can compare caterers later.

Be prepared with numbers.

☐ Come prepared for the appointment with a firm budget in mind.

☐ Bring a general idea of how many guests to expect.

☐ Tell the caterer how far away your guests are coming from. This may cut down on the final number of guests attending your wedding.

Pick your site.

☐ Have your reception site chosen so that the caterer can figure out what you will need. In some cases, the caterer can help you find a site.

Know the type of wedding you plan to have.

☐ Think out the theme, style, and mood of your wedding before talking to the caterer.

Coordinate the catering style and food to the site.

☐ Be sure the caterer matches the reception site in style as well as in menu suggestions.

An appropriate menu for the time of day.

☐ Decide what time of day your reception will be so the caterer can plan an appropriate menu.

☐ Ask the caterer to suggest a suitable menu, whether breakfast, brunch, cocktails, or dinner.

Plan for the number of guests.

☐ Discuss the kind of menu suitable for the number of guests you expect.

☐ Discuss the maximum number of people the caterer is equipped to handle. Is there a minimum?

Favorite dish.

☐ Ask specifically for the dish the chef does best.

Personalize your menu.

☐ In your discussion with the caterer, try to judge whether the caterer is willing to personalize your wedding.

Look for new ideas.

☐ Be sure to ask the caterer for any general or specific menu and serving suggestions.

How much help?

☐ Find out the ratio of waiters to guests.

Table appointments are important.

☐ Talk about the type of linens, long or short table skirts, fabric, plastic, or paper, as well as serving dishes, candlesticks, and so on.

Beverages at the reception.

☐ Talk to the caterer about the types of beverages usually served at the reception.

Estimating the amount of beverages.

☐ The quantity of drinks consumed often depends on the time of year, kind of reception, and hour of the day. People drink more if the weather is warm or if the reception is held in the evening.

☐ Ask your caterer to help estimate quantities. The caterer should take into consideration the type of appetizers served (for instance, whether the appetizers are salty) and the menu itself.

Champagne, anyone?

☐ Sparkling wine, usually called champagne, is sometimes served throughout the reception.

Champagne served with the wedding cake.

☐ Some weddings pour champagne only during the toasting and cake cutting time. Ask your supplier for a dessert champagne.

The open bar.

☐ Many times champagne will be served with the cake, but in the meantime the guests have access to an open bar. Generally you specify your own selection of cocktails.

Serving of beverages.

☐ Find out if the beverages will be served from a stationary or rolling bar.

- ☐ Decide whether the waiter should take drink orders after guests are seated for dinner.
- ☐ Find out how many bartenders will be serving. It's important to have adequate service to make sure guests won't have to stand in long lines waiting for their orders.

Other sources can give you an estimating rule of thumb.

- ☐ You can double-check your caterer's estimate of quantities by asking a reputable liquor store for their recommendations.

More is better than less.

- ☐ When estimating beverages, it's better to order too much then too little. Ask your beverage supplier if unopened bottles may be returned.

Offer a choice.

- ☐ Be sure to offer a choice of nonalcoholic beverages to your guests as well as alcoholic beverages. Consider the preferences of your guests.

Chilling beverages.

- ☐ Ask the caterer about methods of chilling beverages. Plastic tubs or pails prevent leakage and stains.

Cost per person.

- ☐ Generally caterers offer "per-person" reception costs. Ask if the price varies for type of reception (buffet or sit-down dinner), and the entrée served (chicken or beef).

Separate packages.

- ☐ Sometimes the cocktail hour is included in the total price, and sometimes it is considered a separate package.

Site needs.

- ☐ Discuss whether the caterer has any special needs because of the site chosen that are not included in the total cost of the site.

The deposit.

☐ Once you decide on a caterer, a deposit is required. Before signing the contract, find out if the deposit is returnable if a reasonable amount of time is given. Is there a penalty for cancellation?

☐ What is the cutoff date for cancellation?

Final payment.

☐ When is the balance of the payment due?

Tips and gratuities.

☐ Find out if tips are included in the catering package, how much they are, and whom the tips are intended for.

☐ Make sure that your guests are not expected to tip.

Final guest counts.

☐ Most caterers need a final guest count about a week before the wedding date. Get as precise a count as possible. Extra plates increase the total expenses.

Additional factors to weigh in the catering decision.

☐ Ask for references from the last five receptions that your caterer served. Specify the last five customers; don't let the caterer pick names at random. Be sure to call all the names.

☐ Look at any pictures of parties that the caterer has done recently.

☐ Ask if you may visit one of the caterer's receptions. If not, then ask if you can see the preparations beforehand.

☐ Be sure that the caterer carries basic liability insurance, otherwise you may end up paying for any problems.

Pace the reception.

☐ Plan the flow of the reception with the caterer. You want one event to run into another without any holdups or long waiting periods.

Buffet serving table arrangement.

☐ If you are serving buffet style, ask the caterer to diagram the serving dishes on the buffet table. Make sure there are enough tables to serve all the guests in a reasonable amount of time; you don't want to keep people waiting in long lines.

Opening beverage bottles.

☐ Make sure the staff doesn't open beverage bottles un-necessarily ... they should wait until one bottle is finish-ed before opening another one.

Service attire.

☐ You can suggest what the catering help should wear ... tuxedoes or short jackets, white or black, or casual attire such as white shirts, slacks, and sneakers.

9.
Wedding Cake

Choosing the cake.

☐ White cake is traditional, but the trend is toward choosing any flavor of cake that your taste buds favor. Chocolate, carrot, banana, lemon, or fruitcake are all tasty possibilities.

Cake layer filling.

☐ The filling can be as varied as the cake itself. Try cream fillings, fruit fillings, or marzipan between layers.

Alternate filling and cake flavors.

☐ Solve any differences of opinion between you and the groom by alternating cake layers and filling. For example, order a three-tiered cake featuring chocolate, lemon, and strawberry flavors.

The cake top.

☐ The topmost tier of the wedding cake is taken home, stored in the freezer, and enjoyed on the first anniversary.

Use flowers for cake toppers.

☐ Flowers are replacing the traditional bride and groom figures as cake toppers. Whether you use fresh flowers to carry through the bridal bouquet theme or spun sugar flowers that taste as good as they look, you'll be sure to get raves of appreciation.

Safety check.

☐ Be sure any flowers or greens you use for the cake aren't poisonous. Check with your florist.

Theme the cake topper.

☐ Use the cake topper to carry out the theme of your wedding. Try sugared grapes and ivy for a Renaissance theme, fresh daisies for a springtime wedding, or flashing sparklers for a July 4 wedding date.

Personalize the cake topper figures.

☐ Paint small wedding cake figures to match each wedding attendant's hair and eye coloring, as well as their wedding attire.

Unusual cake toppers.

☐ An unexpected cake topper will grab everyone's attention. For instance, use a miniature version of whatever you're interested in: antique cars, bicycles, or boats.

Traditional cake toppers.

☐ For the traditionalists, there are cherubs, wedding bells, hearts, or lovebirds as symbolic cake toppers. These can be of crystal, china, spun sugar, or plastic.

Cake topper sentiment.

☐ Any sentimental topper will draw favorable comment. Use a duplicate of your parent's wedding cake topper. Or use an object that has meaning for you as a couple: a shell from the beach or pine cones from your mountain hiking trip.

The traditional layer cake.

☐ You'll want to consider the shape of your cake, too. Wedding cakes are usually round, square, or heart-shaped tiers. The layers are either set directly on top of one another or they are separated by bakery pillars or upside-down, stemmed glasses.

Alternative cake shapes.

☐ Wedding cakes can be simple round or rectangular sheet cakes. The sheet cake can be designed and cut to fit a theme. You can make the cake look like the shape of your state, a castle, or a prayerbook.

Cake decorations.

☐ Traditional cakes have a white icing pattern sometimes decorated with gold or silver icing beads.

☐ For a variation try a swirl of colored icing, that matches your wedding colors.

☐ Use fresh or silk blossoms on the sides of the cake to blend with the cake topper. You can stick the stems of fresh flowers into tiny florists' water vials.

☐ For an ultra-high-fashion look, have your baker decorate your cake with gold leaf. Use it sparingly, because it's expensive.

☐ Consider tiny white satin ribbons, ivy leaves, or pearl ropes to adorn your cake.

Cake color theme.

☐ Choose colors from your wedding color theme for the cake icing and decorations.

Seasonal cakes.

☐ Follow the seasons with your choice of cake; spice for fall, fruitcake for winter, pistachio for spring, and lemon with raspberry puree filling for summer.

Heritage cakes.

☐ Give a nod to your heritage with an Italian cheesecake, a French Choux à la Creme (a pyramid of small puff pastries filled with cream), an English pound cake, a Scandinavian Kronsekage (flat round ring cakes of different sizes stacked to form a pyramid), or an Austrian Sacher Torte (a chocolate cake served with whipped cream).

Theme cake styles.

☐ Style your cake in the same fashion as your wedding. Try a chocolate-and-white layer cake for a sophisticated black-and-white theme, a heart-shaped cherry-flavored cake for Valentine's Day, or a walnut or banana cake for a country-style wedding. (See *Wedding Plans: 50 Unique Themes For the Wedding of Your Dreams* for a variety of personalized wedding theme ideas. Write to Brighton Publications, Inc., P.O. Box 12706, New Brighton, MN 55112, for ordering information.)

The-groom's cake.

☐ Many weddings have groom cakes. These can be baked in any size, shape, or flavor. The traditional groom cake is fruitcake cut into small pieces and boxed for take-home mementos. Many bakers do not provide the small boxes, so you'll have to find them at a party-supply store.

Extra cakes.

☐ Order extra cakes to make sure all the guests will be served. Set one flower basket–shaped cake on each side of the wedding cake. Ice in a lattice design, and set fresh flowers in the top of each cake basket. This is a lovely alternative to a sheet cake.

Cake and cookies.

☐ Cookies are often served on the same table as the cake. Use your family's favorite recipe or cut the cookies into wedding symbols such as hearts. Then again, you can make cookies to express an interest: musical notes for music, shamrocks for your honeymoon destination.

Confections.

☐ Wedding reception confections can include decorative mints, marzipan candy, candies known for the region (such as saltwater taffy in the Northeast), or long-stemmed chocolate roses.

Finding the right bakery.

☐ Word-of-mouth recommendations are best when selecting a baker. Ask your friends and relatives for their recommendations.

☐ If you're on your own with no one to help you, then stop in at two or three bakeries and look at their samples and photos.

Delivering the wedding cake.

☑ Find out if the bakery will deliver to your reception site and at a time convenient for you. Will the delivery cost extra? Keep in mind that you'll need to have the cake delivered at a time when someone will be able to let the delivery people into the reception room.

☐ If you have friends deliver the cake, at least two dependable people should be working together. It's still a risky business, however.

Holiday wedding dates.

☐ Should your wedding date fall on a major holiday, the cake will be baked ahead of time. You will have the responsibility of delivering the cake to the reception.

Choosing the bakery.

☐ Before choosing a bakery, compare the selection of cakes available, the bakery's willingness to please you, and the cost.

Cake servings.

☐ A three-tiered cake, including a small, fourth tier for a memento, plus two quarter (9 x 14-inch) sheet cakes or two 8-inch round cakes will serve 200 guests.

Other sources for wedding cakes.

☐ Other sources can supply you with a wedding cake. Try the hotel, caterer, a one-person in-home operation, or a friend or relative. Don't bake your own unless it's a small cake and you can do it several days in advance.

Number of cake servings you will need.

☐ When you talk to the bakery, know at least a rough estimate of cake servings you will need.

Cake preference.

☐ Sort out cake and icing preferences among you, the groom,

and your families before you start talking to the bakery.

Bring samples of your cake preference.

☐ If you have any color, style, or other theme preferences, bring pictures, swatches, and sketches with you.

Final taste.

☐ Taste a sample of the cake before confirming the order. Your taste buds will tell you if you made the right selection.

The written contract.

☐ Complete a written contract specifying decorations, the shape, size, and type of cake, as well as the wedding day, delivery date, time, and address.

Keep the wedding cake in a cool room.

☐ Here's a sad, but true, story: A couple's wedding cake was baked just as ordered, delivered well ahead of time, and set safely on the cake table. However, the cake was frosted with whipped cream and the room was warm. Just before the first guests arrived, the hotel caterer found the top tier on the floor. The whipped cream had melted and the top had slid to the floor. So one more reminder: Keep the wedding cake in a cool room, away from heat or sun.

10.
Wedding
Photographs
& Video

Shop early for a phographer.

□ Start looking for a photographer as soon as you've set the date. Good wedding photographers are booked almost a year in advance.

Ask for recommendations.

□ Talk to friends and relatives who have had a recent wedding in their family. Ask them whether they liked a particular photographer, and why.

Check ads in newspapers and local magazines.

□ Find an experienced wedding photographer through ads catering to the wedding market. They're the ones most likely to know the wedding procedures and can anticipate the best camera shots.

Compare photographers.

□ Compare the photographer's ability to work with people, as well as the pricing structure. The photographer should get the candids as quickly and discreetly as possible.

Technical work.

□ Check the photographer's technical work. Are the pictures in focus? Are most of the shots inside or outdoors in natural settings?

Sample work.

□ Ask to see sample wedding albums as well as miscellaneous pictures.

Shop for quality.

□ Look for a photographer who will make your wedding party members appear natural, see to it that important moments are captured, and record the natural sequence of wedding day events.

Photographer's fees.

☐ Photographers charge one of three ways: by the "package," by the number of pictures taken, or by the hour.

Photo package concerns.

☐ Does the photo package price include individual prints or proofs only? Find out who picks the pictures—you or the photographer.

☐ Often a wedding album is part of the package.

One chance for wedding photo memories.

☐ Select the best photographer possible; if necessary, choose fewer pictures for your album.

Put the younger guests to work.

☐ Give your young cousins, nieces, or nephews an inexpensive camera to use at the reception. You're sure to end up with a unique pictorial perspective of your wedding.

The typical photo package.

☐ Most couples purchase one large 8 x 10-inch portrait of bride and groom, a set of previews or proofs from which to choose, an album of large prints, and a gift album of smaller prints for the parents.

Other uses for wedding pictures.

☐ Photographs can be used for holiday greeting cards, especially if the wedding is in late summer or fall.

Photos taken at the receiving line.

☐ Some wedding couples have pictures taken of everyone at the receiving line so they can enclose snaps with each thank-you note.

Photo-taking sessions.

☐ Don't let after-wedding photo sessions last too long. Usually guests will be waiting for you to begin the wedding festivities.

Pose for the wedding portrait before the wedding.

☐ Sometimes the wedding portrait can be taken ahead of time, reserving more time for you to enjoy your guests.

Photography sites.

☐ Think twice when the photographer wants to take you and your wedding party to a natural setting for pictures. Grassy slopes and dirt paths can ruin the bottom of long dresses and delicately dyed wedding shoes. Keep in mind that you still have to look nice for the ceremony or reception.

Photographer's assistant.

☐ Ask a friend to assist the photographer to make sure that he or she gets shots of special moments and friends.

Make a list of your most-wanted photos.

☐ Typical photos taken before the ceremony are of bride with mother, father, and attendants; bride getting into the car; groom; and groom with best man.

☐ Photos at the wedding can include bride and groom coming up the aisle, ceremony moments, soloist and organist, alter or canopy during the ceremony, exchanging of vows, and the ring ceremony.

☐ Photos before the reception often are of bride and groom together, bride's and groom's hands, bride and groom with parents and wedding party, and other people with the bride and groom.

☐ Photos at the reception usually include the wedding couple arriving, the receiving line, buffet table, first wedding dance as a couple and with parents, the cake table, cutting the cake, feeding each other the cake, bride and groom toasting, throwing and catching the bouquet, groom taking off the bride's garter, throwing and catching the garter, wedding party decorating the car, bride and groom leaving, and guests throwing rice.

Specify time of photographer's arrival and departure.

☐ Don't let this happen at your wedding: The mother of the bride helped a daughter settle her children with the babysitter before going on to the reception. In the meantime, the photographer, wanting to leave the wedding for one reason or another, persuaded the bride and groom to cut the cake so he could take pictures. When the mother arrived, she found she had completely missed the cake-cutting ceremony.

Photographers's contract details.

☐ Written price quotation.
☐ Time of arrival and departure.
☐ Number of pictures in color. In black-and-white.
☐ Number of previews or proofs to choose from.
☐ Written list of must-have wedding activity photos.
☐ Written list of pictures with guests.
☐ Written list of special instructions or restrictions.
☐ The kind of album that comes with the package.
☐ Procedure for refunding your deposit if the wedding is cancelled or postponed.
☐ Financial arrangements.

Check back with the photographer.

☐ It's a good idea to touch base with the photographer a week or two before the wedding to be sure everyone is clear about the details.

Finding a video professional.

☐ Talk to friends who have had their weddings taped, ask the caterer or wedding consultant for names, or look in the Yellow Pages.

Photo and video package.

☐ Check with your photographer. Some have both a photo and a video package you can purchase.

Video samples.

☐ View work samples of video companies. Look for sound quality, sequence of scenes, lighting, and smoothness of storytelling.

Video format.

☐ Although VHS is the most popular video format, you can choose Beta or 8 mm. Make sure the VCR you're going to use is the same format as your tapes.

Optional additions.

☐ Extra charges often include editing, title, voice-over, and interviews. You might want to suggest your own questions for interviews.

Total package cost.

☐ The total cost of the video will depend on the length of the tape, whether sound was recorded, the amount of editing done, and extras such as background music and titles.

Video site preplanning.

☐ Take the video crew to the wedding site and discuss where the camera will be located, any lighting problems, and so on.

Marriage site restrictions.

☐ Before signing a contract, make sure your church or

synagogue will allow videotaping during the ceremony, and if they do, where they will allow the camera to be set up.

Contract considerations.

☐ The contract should specify what the video company will provide and the fee required. It should also state arrival and departure times, number of cameras, amount of editing to be done, and the date and time.

Coordinate video and photography.

☐ Coordinate the video activities with the still photographer. One solution is to write out a time script for each one.

Tapes as gifts.

☐ Consider having duplicate tapes made. They make a wonderful thank-you gift for both sets of parents.

Last thought.

☐ Remember: You have just one chance to get lasting pictures of this memorable day. Make sure you know what you want, and then go about finding the person you're most certain will provide the best pictures. In the end, the responsibility is yours, so take the time to choose a good photographer.

Music &
Entertainment
11.

The music plays on.

☐ After-dinner dance music is now the norm for many weddings.

☐ Background music brightens the cocktail hour and dinner.

☐ Entrances by the bride and groom and the beginning of activities such as throwing the bouquet is often begun with a flourish of music.

☐ Marching music can accompany the wedding party's entrance to the reception.

Start the band search early.

☐ It's important to engage the band as soon as possible, especially if you want a popular or special type of band.

Confirmation.

☐ Confirm the wedding date, time, and site with the band leader.

There are a variety of musical possibilities.

☐ Try big bands, disc jockeys with taped music, classical trios, woodwind ensembles, string quartets, harpist, piano player, strolling violin, guitar, or accordian player.

Alternatives to a big-name band.

☐ The most popular alternative to popular bands is the disc jockey with prerecorded music.

☐ Find a group of amateur musicians from a community center or from a local university or college.

☐ Try out the local high school band.

☐ Settle for smaller numbers, and hire a trio or combo.

Check with your reception site manager.

☐ Some catering halls, clubs, and hotels allow only their house bands to play.

Finding good musicians.

☐ A special recommendation from friends, relatives, or newlyweds is the most reliable way to find good musicians.

☐ Look in the Yellow Pages for the musician's union, and ask for their recommendations.

☐ Consult wedding planners and caterers for their ideas.

☐ Consider musicians who advertise in local wedding guides or newspaper sections. They will be the most attuned to weddings.

Know your guests' preferences.

☐ Keep your guest list in mind when choosing a band. Be sure the kind of music the band plays will be enjoyed by most of your guests.

Band breaks.

☐ Have a clear understanding of how many breaks the band will take and the length of time each break lasts.

Special requests.

☐ You may have certain songs in mind to be played for the special dances. Find out if the band takes special requests.

Announcements.

☐ Discuss the bandleader's willingness and experience in making announcements. You may want the bandleader to announce the first wedding dance.

Band members' attire.

☐ Consider the band members' dress. Will their attire complement your style of wedding?

Sample the band's music.

☐ Audition the band when they are playing the tunes you expect them to play at your wedding. If possible, try to catch the band when they are playing in a room about the same size as the one in which your reception will be held.

Date and time band is to play.

☐ In the contract, be sure to include the correct date and time the band is to play, as well as how long they are to play.

Bandleader.

☐ If you hired the band because of its big-name bandleader, make sure the contract specifies the leader's name.

Playing band members.

☐ It is important to specify in the contract the number of band members who will be playing.

Band members' attire.

☐ Mentioning the attire of the band members in the contract will ensure that they won't show up in shorts and sneakers for your black-tie wedding.

Band breaks.

☐ In the contract, specify the number and length of breaks.

Special equipment needs.

☐ Put down in writing any special equipment needs of the band.

Payment.

☐ Specify the complete terms of payment in the contract.

Pre-wedding details.

☐ Provide any special equipment needed, such as platform, stands, and electrical outlets.

☐ Well before the wedding date, supply the bandleader with a list of special requests.

☐ Prepare a list of any fanfares you'll need for traditional wedding activities.

☐ Give the bandleader a list of announcements and introductions. For example, you'll want the leader to announce the special dances and to pronounce each name correctly.

Give some thought to the sequence of special dances.

☐ The first dance belongs to the bride and groom.

☐ The second dance, the bride dances with her father, and the groom dances with the bride's mother.

☐ The third dance, the bride dances with the groom's father, and the groom dances with his mother.

☐ The fourth dance, everyone in the wedding party dances.

☐ The fifth dance, everybody dances.

Special song requests.

☐ Discuss with the bandleader appropriate songs that might be played. For instance, your special song could be played for the first dance, and a show tune could be played when you are dancing with your parents.

Special hints that will help both you and the band.

☐ Provide a small room and light refreshments for the band during breaks.

☐ Give the bandleader the site manager's name and telephone number so special equipment arrangements can be made.

☐ If the site is small, ask the band to use less percussion, fewer amplifiers, and lower speaker volume.

☐ If you can't afford to pay overtime, instruct the band to play wind-down music 15 minutes before the end of the contract period.

Special effects.

☐ Some bands offer an option of smoke or bubbles with their music.

☐ Special light effects or light shows can be coordinated with the band's music.

When the musicians are late . . .

☐ Scan the guest list. Is there a piano player in the group?

☐ Substitute activity. Ask the juggler who was to perform during the band's break to open the festivities.

☐ Lengthen the cocktail hour until the dinner musicians show up.

☐ Read the contract. There may be contingency plans you can follow.

If the musicians don't arrive . . .

☐ Have cassettes and a tape player ready in the wings, where you can get your hands on them quickly.

☐ Look in the Yellow Pages for a disc jockey who is willing to play taped music at the last minute.

☐ Put on a happy face and turn up the radio . . . loud!

Music your guests will enjoy.

☐ Engage one band that can play a wide range of music, or perhaps book two bands: one for the young people and one for the older set.

☐ Consider big-band classics, contemporary pop, classical, regional, or ethnic music.

Match the music to the wedding style.

☐ Keep the music low-key if the reception is simple. Engage a piano player, harpist, woodwind ensemble, strolling violinist, guitarist, or accordian player.

Special dances can influence your choice of musicians.

☐ You should know if the family tradition dictates dancing the polka, Irish jig, Italian tarantella, or the Jewish horah; choose the band accordingly.

Entertainment while the band takes a break.

☐ While the band takes breaks, change the pace of the festivities with short acts like a mime, juggler, comedian, magician, caricature artist, or balloon artist.

Wedding themes can help you choose the right kind of music.

☐ Rock through the night with a fifties theme and a jukebox.

☐ A Renaissance theme demands lutes and singers.

☐ Regional themes require a round of square dancing or Virginia reels.

☐ Ethnic themes can embrace each family's music and dance.

☐ Contemporary weddings will enjoy a combination of popular music and laser light entertainment.

☐ Holiday theme weddings, such as the Fourth of July, will sparkle with fireworks.

Wedding sites can be entertainment in themselves.

☐ Let the site entertain your guests. Select garden or parklike settings, rent ranches, ski lodges or historical mansions, or invite your guests to the honeymoon setting. . . Florida, Bermuda, or Hawaii.

Transportation can add to your guests' entertainment.

☐ Provide buggy rides, boat rides, classic car rides, limousine rides, school bus or tour bus rides, hot air balloon rides—anything that will reflect your wedding's style

Finding good entertainment.

☐ Look for entertainment that entertains you. If you like it, your guests will probably will, too.

☐ Find your entertainment through personal recommendations, the Yellow Pages, local schools or through wedding consultants and caterers.

☐ Try to audition any acts before the wedding.

Signing the contract.

☐ Remember to put everything down in writing in the contract.

One final thought.

☐ Choose reception music and entertainment that reflects you, your guests, and your wedding style.

12.
Wedding
Flowers

Window shopping.

☐ Scan the windows of flower shops. If you like their displays, chances are you'll like their suggestions for your wedding.

Personal recommendations.

☐ Ask friends and acquaintances to recommend any flower shops they particularly like.

Albums and pictures.

☐ Look at florists' albums and pictures to see the kind of work they have done for other weddings.

Talk to florists.

☐ Once you've narrowed your list of possible florists a bit, talk to florists individually to get an idea of what each can do for you and, of course, what the costs will be.

Compare florists.

☐ Compare written estimates, willingness to please, and how innovative and creative each florist is before you make your final decision.

Help the florist to help you.

☐ The best help you can give your florist is to bring a magazine picture, snapshot, or sketch of your wedding dress and bridesmaids' dresses with you. Bring fabric swatches, too.

☐ If you like certain flowers or styles of bouquets, bring those pictures or sketches along, too.

Adequate time.

☐ Give the florist plenty of time. Ideally your first contact with the florist should be at least three to four months in advance of the wedding.

Decide how much you want to spend.

☐ Try to come up with a budget so the florist can work toward staying within these limits.

Decide on your priorities.

☐ Do you want the flower focus to be on the ceremony or reception, the bouquets and boutonnieres, or the decorative pew flowers and centerpieces?

Be flexible.

☐ Do yourself a favor: Plan to be flexible. Some flowers you like may be out of season, too exotic, or just not available from the wholesalers. Trust your florist to come up with good alternatives.

Flower budget guidelines.

☐ Experts say to estimate 10 to 15 percent of your total wedding budget for wedding flowers. If you want fresh floral centerpieces, you should count on spending 15 to 20 persent of your total budget on flowers.

Cutting flower costs.

☐ It's a plain and simple fact: The fewer the bridesmaids, the fewer bouquets that have to be purchased.

☐ Ask your florist to offer selections of flowers that will be in season at the time of your wedding.

☐ Rather than a bouquet of fresh flowers, perhaps your flower girl can carry a small basket of dried flowers or rose petals that she can drop in the aisle.

☐ Be creative in cutting flower costs. For example, use *one* blossom of the birthday flower of each bridesmaid and surround it with greenery and ribbon.

☐ If you want to limit the flower budget, don't plan a wedding around Valentine's Day, Mother's Day, or the local high school prom. Fresh flowers are at their most expensive at these times, and your florist will be extra busy around these dates, too.

Cluster bouquets.

☐ Bride and bridesmaids should carry round cluster bouquets low enough to show the details of the gown but at a height that is a natural carrying position.

Cascade bouquets.

☐ Long and flowing cascade bouquets are usually held in front.

Arm bouquets.

☐ Arm bouquets, tied bunches of flowers with stems intact, are carried naturally in the curve of the arm. The arm should be resting at hip level.

Single stemmed flowers.

☐ Single stems can be clutched and held in the front or carried naturally at the side, with the flowers down.

Wreaths.

☐ Wreaths can be held down at the side or in front with both hands.

Flower baskets.

☐ Baskets of flowers can be carried at the side with one hand.

Boutonnieres.

☐ Boutonnieres are pinned to the left lapel with the pin underneath so the pin can't be seen.

Corsages.

☐ Corsages should be worn on the left shoulder, with stems down, as the flowers grow.

Headpieces.

☐ Headpieces should be measured for fit with the hair done in the style in which it is to be worn for the wedding.

Bridal flowers.

☐ White is the traditional color for flowers in the bridal bouquet. Favorite white flowers include roses, orchids, gardenias, chrysanthemums, carnations, and stephanotis. An accent color is sometimes introduced.

The bouquet toss.

☐ If you want to save your bouquet, but you also want to enjoy the traditional bouquet toss, order a duplicate bouquet.

☐ Another alternative is to have a portion of your bouquet break away for the toss. The center of the bouquet is retained as a keepsake.

☐ Include a charm with your names and wedding date inscribed in the bouquet you toss to your bridesmaids.

Preserving your bouquet.

☐ Air dry the flowers on a shelf for four to six weeks. Then place the bouquet under a plastic or glass display dome.

☐ Some flowers, such as daisies and Queen Anne's lace, can be pressed and used to decorate the wedding album or framed wedding photographs.

☐ Save the petals of fragrant flowers to make a potpourri.

☐ Root a green plant such as ivy and grow the wedding green in your new home.

Lapel flowers for men.

☐ Rosebuds are traditional, fragrant lapel flowers in white, pink, red, or yellow.

☐ Carnations are lovely fresh flowers that can be dyed to blend with almost any color scheme.

☐ Ixias are slender, delicate flowers in pale shades of lavender, pink, and white.

☐ Mini-cymbidium orchids hold up very well and come in every shade except blue.

☐ Alstroemeria are lilylike and come in shades of reddish purple, yellow, and white.

☐ Alliums look like a cluster of blossoms and come in lavender, pink, or white.

For the mothers.

☐ Order corsages that are equal for both mothers, but personalize them with different colors.

Different flowers and shapes create different looks.

☐ Use exotic greenery and fewer flowers to provide a dramatic effect.

☐ Nosegays of garden flowers offer a sweet, innocent look.

☐ Opalescent ribbons and bows add a certain sophistication.

☐ Heirloom jewelry wound among the flowers brings a special, sentimental meaning to the bouquet.

Bouquet size.

☐ The size of the bouquet should be in proportion to the height and dress style of the person carrying it.

Blend and soften the bouquet's colors.

☐ Since most flowers won't match the dresses exactly, blend and soften the colors in the bouquet by adding a touch of white baby's breath.

Ways to complement hard-to-match dress colors.

☐ If the attendants' dresses are of a color that is very hard to match, as are some blues, choose colors that are opposite on the color wheel. Flowers in the orange-yellow family will complement those difficult blues.

Duplicate your mother's wedding bouquet.

☐ Bring a picture of your mother's wedding bouquet to your florist and have it copied in either fresh or silk flowers.

Flowers in bouquets can hold special meaning.

☐ Here are some flowers and their meanings: white chrysanthemum—truth; daisy—gentleness; forget-me-not—true love; gardenia—untold love; ivy—fidelity; lilac—humility; rose—everlasting love.

☐ If you choose a flower for its special meaning, be sure to let your guests know, perhaps in the ceremony booklets given to your guests.

Potpourri sachets.

☐ Attach a potpourri sachet to each bridesmaid's bouquet for a lasting, fragrant remembrance.

Single, stemmed flowers.

☐ Set a basket of single, stemmed flowers within easy reach of your guests for wedding mementos.

Rosebud favors.

☐ Instruct the younger members of the wedding party to hand out a lapel rosebud to each guest as a wedding favor.

Parents' thank-you flowers.

☐ Order a bouquet of flowers to be sent to your parents' home the day after the wedding as a heartfelt thank-you.

Advantages of fresh flowers.

☐ Fresh flowers impart a look of luxury and freshness to any gathering.

☐ The fragrance of fresh flowers adds a sensory delight to the festivities.

- [ ] Fresh flowers have a natural look and feel, unlike the static stiffness of silk flowers.
- [ ] Some prefer the look of fresh flowers in the wedding photos.
- [ ] Fresh flowers are traditional.

Advantages of silk flowers.

- [ ] Bouquets and arrangements can be prepared well ahead of time. It's one less detail to worry about on the day of the wedding.
- [ ] Flowers can be dyed to match bridesmaids' dresses.
- [ ] Silk bouquets can be made up ahead of time for pre-wedding photography sessions and saved without worry for the wedding later.
- [ ] Attendants' bouquets can be rearranged into floral displays as mementos of the wedding day.
- [ ] The cost of silk flowers is just a little more than that of fresh flowers, especially if the fresh flowers to be ordered are out of season.

The versatility of flowers.

- [ ] Besides the usual bouquets and arrangements, flowers can appear as pew markers, door decorations, cake toppers, favors for guests, headpieces, candle centerpieces, and leis for the wedding party and guests.

Flowers for the ceremony.

- [ ] Flowers should complement the church as well as the style of the wedding.
- [ ] Use light-colored flowers for churches with dark interior walls. Frame the flowers with dark green leaves if the church has a light interior.
- [ ] The arrangements should be placed high so they can be seen by everyone.

Cutting ceremony flower costs.

- ☐ To cut flower cost, use more ribbons, bows, and greenery, especially for pew markers.

- ☐ Most bouquets or plants used at the ceremony site can be transported to the reception area.

- ☐ Share expenses with another wedding couple if they are to be married the same day.

- ☐ Rent potted plants and flowers and return them after the ceremony. This can also be done for the reception.

- ☐ If your budget demands that you choose between ceremony and reception, purchase flowers for the reception area. During the ceremony, the wedding attire is often color enough, and all attention is focused on the proceedings. Also, remember, you and your guests will be spending the most time at the reception.

13.
Wedding
Attire

Shop several stores.

☐ When shopping for bridal and bridesmaids dresses, try on several styles, even though it seems everyone comes back to the first dress they see. Remember a salesperson's first priority is to sell. Don't let anyone talk you into buying anything you don't really like.

Before sewing your dress.

☐ If you plan to sew your own wedding gown, before choosing your pattern, go to bridal shops and departments and try on dresses to find the style and colors that best suits you.

Take along a companion.

☐ It's a good idea to take someone with you, like a mother, older sister, or good friend, to keep you from overspending. Besides keeping you sensible, they can take notes like mad on the dress style, length, fabric, and color that best suits you.

Choose the correct size.

☐ After you've chosen the style of your dress, be careful you don't get fitted for a size too large. When the dress arrives, it will need to be refitted, and you could get stuck with a steep alteration charge.

Wedding dress colors.

☐ Popular wedding dress colors are white, ivory, and champagne. Pale blue or yellow is sometimes used under lace or cutwork.

Choose the dress for the season.

☐ As you're selecting your dresses, imagine yourself in the season that your wedding will take place. Select the color, weight, and style of dress that will fit the season. Otherwise you may be wearing a heavy winter dress on a 90-degree day.

Consider each bridesmaid.

☐ Before choosing the bridesmaids' dresses, think a little about each bridesmaid's personality, body shape, and coloring. Try to get a style that will flatter all of them.

Let the bridesmaid select the style.

☐ If all the bridesmaids are of different shapes and sizes, buy the same fabric but let each bridesmaid select the style.

Out-of-town bridesmaids.

☐ Take pictures of two or three different dresses and send them to the bridesmaids. They may find a dress of the same style in their shopping area. If they can't, they can still get a feel for the dress and give you their opinions.

A dress for all occasions.

☐ Some people feel that the bridesmaid's dress should be of a style that can be worn for other occasions. *But it's not going to work*! Do yourself and your bridesmaids a favor and select a dress style with just the wedding in mind. You can be practical in other areas.

Bridesmaid dress party idea.

☐ Old or vintage bridesmaids' dresses are just the thing for a great party idea. Special all-women parties are arranged around the theme of "Wear Your Bridesmaid Dress."

Evening dress department.

☐ One possibility when shopping for bridesmaids' and mothers' dresses is to check the evening dress department. An evening dress may do just as well and cost half as much.

Finding the best white.

☐ Some color consultants can find the best white for you by matching the bridal dress color to your tooth color, the skin area behind the ear, or the color of your palms.

Wearing white.

☐ If white is not your best color, choose colors in the bridal bouquet that compliment you. Then if the bouquet is held high at the waist, the flowers will soften the effect of the white dress.

Line a white lace dress.

☐ The underlining of a white lace dress can be chosen for its compatibility with your skin tone and bring the dress closer to a color that is right for you.

One color, different shades.

☐ If you must have the bridesmaids' dresses in your favorite color, then allow each maid to choose the shade of that color that looks best on her.

One style, different colors.

☐ Sometimes the bridesmaids are so different in their skin coloring that the best decision is to choose one dress style but in colors that flatters each bridesmaid.

Bridal dress fabrics.

☐ Taffeta and satin are favorite choices for bridal dresses. Organza is often used for overskirts, while dotted swiss is chosen for garden weddings, and cotton gets the nod for country weddings.

Lace trim.

☐ Lace adds an extra dimension to the bridal dress. You can choose hand-finished or machine-made lace. Hand-finished lace will be more expensive.

Shop with someone who has sewing experience.

☐ Take someone who has some knowledge of sewing with

you to shop for your dress. She can check the care taken in sewing the buttons, loops, zippers, closings, and seams. She can also tell if laces and beads are glued rather than sewn. If glue or paste is used, the dress should cost less.

Reasons why some dresses are more expensive.

☐ When a dress is made of natural or imported fabric, it will be more expensive. Great attention to detailing will also cost more.

Seasonal dresses.

☐ Spring and summer weddings call for airy, fluffy, lightweight fabric. Choose pastel dresses in organza, chiffon, or lightweight satin.

☐ Satin dresses with a longer sleeve are appropriate for fall. Pick gold, wine, or russet colors for the bridesmaids' dresses.

☐ Velvets shine at Christmastime. Choose red, dark green, ice blue, perhaps in a style trimmed with fur.

☐ Around Valentine's Day the bridal dress should be of heavy satin or taffeta. Use red crepe bridesmaids' dresses as the holiday accent.

Cutting cost with fabric substitutions.

☐ Substitute polyester taffeta for silk peau de soie, polyester for silk, and polyester chiffon for silk chiffon.

Final dress fitting.

☐ Wear the undergarments you plan to wear on the wedding day, as well as the shoes (or shoes with the same heel height), for the final dress fitting.

Losing weight.

☐ Avoid the mistake of thinking you're going to lose weight when you're being fitted for dresses. This advice holds true for the bridesmaids, the mothers, and probably the groom, too.

Finding an inexpensive bridal dress.

☐ Look in the newspapers for warehouse bridal sales or sample dress sales. Also, think about renting a dress. Better yet, find a seamstress or sew your own dress.

Working with a seamstress.

☐ Schedule a visit with your seamstress before going to a fabric store. Get acquainted with each other. Bring pictures of dresses you like and ask the seamstress for an opinion about dress design, fabric, accessories, ornamentation, and the amount of fabric needed.

☐ In most cases, the seamstress should be willing to go with you to pick out your fabric. Take advantage of the help.

Mix patterns to achieve a personal look.

☐ Sewing or having a dress sewn gives you exactly the style of dress you want. Combine pattern tops, bottoms, and sleeves for your own personal look.

Muslin sample.

☐ Always sew a muslin sample, especially for the top of the dress. This will assure you of a good fit.

Use new pins.

☐ Buy a new box of straight pins before sewing on the dress fabric. New pins will help avoid snags.

Sewing thread.

☐ Regular dual-duty thread is fine for sewing satin or taffeta fabric.

Caring for expensive fabric.

☐ When you buy expensive fabric, especially satin, make

sure the fabric is rolled around tubing. Don't let the salesperson fold the fabric and put it in a paper bag. The creases from folding won't be able to be pressed out of the fabric.

Hold fabric taut.

☐ When sewing, hold the fabric taut both behind and ahead of the pressure foot to prevent puckering.

Finished seams.

☐ Seams don't have to be finished off because the dress is worn only once. Finished seams are for clothing that will be worn often.

Dress lining.

☐ Lining the dress is important to hide the bumps and folds of a half slip. The half slip line can show up in photographs, too. With a lining, you needn't worry.

Dress hem.

☐ When hemming the dress, make sure you slip stitch all the way around rather than just tacking. This will prevent your heel from getting caught in the hem and tearing your dress.

Lace appliqués.

☐ Enough appliqués (lace cutouts) can be found from a 1-yard length of 36-inch-wide lace fabric for front, back, and both sleeves.

Pearls and sequins.

☐ If adding pearls and sequins, add them to the lace appliqué before sewing the appliqué to the dress.

Hot irons.

☐ Avoid a hot iron on any of the bridal or bridesmaid fabrics.

Use a dry iron.

☐ *Don't use steam at any time.* Steam may make puckers and water spots on satin and some taffeta. Use a dry iron. Don't overpress. The weight of the satin fabric will pull out most wrinkles.

Pressing seams.

☐ Press seams before opening the seam to relax, meld, and bond the stitches and fabric together. Then, open the seam allowance and press flat.

Hem length.

☐ Hems of the bridal and bridesmaids' dresses should be about the same distance from the floor.

Hem width.

☐ Not only should the dresses be of the same length, but the width of the hems on each dress should be the same. This detail does show up on the group wedding pictures.

Pressing hems.

☐ After hemming the dresses, press the hemming line, not the edge, of the dress.

A pressing mistake.

☐ One bride-to-be and her mother sewed the bridal dress and three bridesmaids dresses themselves. Since they were experienced, the dresses turned out wonderfully. But, when they gave the dresses to the bridesmaids, they neglected to tell them how to press the dresses. One of the bridesmaids showed up on the wedding morning with the bottom edge of the dress pressed into a sharp line, ruining the fullness of the satin skirt in contrast to the others. The point of the story is . . . don't assume anything; give complete and precise instructions to everyone.

The bridal veil.

☐ Keep the veil simple to complement the bridal dress. Don't overdo the veil.

Combs for headpieces.

☐ Before buying the headpiece, check to see if combs are sewn on the ring. If not, you'll have to buy combs and sew them on yourself.

Sew a bridal headpiece.

☐ If you've never sewn before but are somewhat handy with crafts, you can make a bridal headpiece. You'll be able to sew a veil for a third of what it would cost ready made.

☐ Bring a picture of a veil you have in mind to the bridal fabric department. Most stores have instructions for veil making. It's mostly gluing and a little hand stitching to attach the veil to the headpiece. You can add beads, lace, sequins, or pearls.

Fitting headpieces.

☐ Both bride and bridesmaids should decide on a hair style for the wedding day before they choose and fit their head-pieces.

Beauty shop advice.

☐ When you have your hair done for the wedding, bring your personal attendant with you. The beautician can show both of you the best way to wear and secure the bridal veil.

Bridal dress train.

☐ Trains can be bustled, carried with a train carrier hoop, or completely removed.

Bustles.

☐ If your dress doesn't come with a built-in bustle, you can add one. Bustles can be formed by attaching loops on the end of the trains to buttons at the waist. Another way is to attach plastic rings to strips of twill tape sewn on the center and two side seams of the skirt. Then thread ribbons through the rings, pull them tight for the desired bustling effect and tie the ribbon securely.

Should the train be bustled?

☐ The weight, style, and length of train determines whether or not you should bustle.

Ask for bustling advice.

☐ Be sure to ask your salesperson or seamstress to show you and your personal attendant how to bustle the train. It does take practice to make it look just right.

Train carrier hoop.

☐ A short train can be handled with a train carrier hoop. Decorate an 8- or 10-inch windsock frame or metal embroidery hoop with flowers and ribbons. Hang the hoop on your arm and pull the train through.

Detachable trains.

☐ Detachable trains are best. The loops and buttons of the bustle can and usually do get torn off the dress, and then the train is constantly falling to the floor and being stepped on. A detachable train is especially good if you plan to dance at your wedding.

Long trains, small brides.

☐ Petite brides sometimes have a difficult time carrying a long, heavy train. Opt for a train that is short and lightweight.

The flower girl dress.

☐ Dresses for flower girls are usually a younger version of the bridesmaids dresses, or the dress is patterned after the bridal dress.

The ring bearer.

☐ The ring bearer is fitted for his tuxedo at the same time as the groom and attendants.

Groom and attendants.

☐ Cummerbunds and bow ties can be plaid or a solid color to match or blend with a partner's dress. Or, they can be coordinated. For example, gold pin dots on black cummerbunds go nicely with red bridesmaids' dresses.

☐ If the right cummerbund or tie can't be found, they can be sewn.

Wearing your mother's wedding dress.

☐ Because silk lace on older wedding dresses doesn't hold up very well, especially on the bottom of skirts, you may have to replace it.

☐ Missing buttons often can't be replaced because such small buttons can't be found nowadays. You'll have to replace all the buttons. Luckily, the new buttons will still fit the loops.

☐ Twenty to twenty-five years ago, women weren't quite as broad across the shoulders and their arms weren't as heavy as those of women today. Much of the change is due to girls participating in swimming and gymnastics. Whatever the reason, the top of Mom's dress will most likely have to be altered

Cleaning bridal dresses.

☐ Know your cleaners. Do they have experience with wedding dresses? Do they or can they press without steam? Water marks make a lasting stain on some fabrics.

☐ Bring extra beads, pearls, the glue that was used on your dress, and pieces of fabric if you can. The cleaners can test the samples before working on the dress.

Storing bridal dresses.

☐ Buy treated tissue paper from your dry cleaner to wrap your dress in before storing. Some cleaners offer a boxing service.

☐ Store the dress in a controlled temperature environment. Protect it from moths, discoloration, and deterioration.

14.
Marriage
License

Where to apply.

☐ Call the marriage bureau, city hall, or the town clerk to ask about procedures. Every area is different.

Length of time needed to apply before the wedding.

☐ Check the length of time the license will be valid.

☐ Blood tests results, which some states require, may take up to thirty days to get back from the lab.

☐ In some states there is a waiting period after obtaining the license before the marriage can take place.

Know your state's health requirements.

☐ Blood tests to check for venereal disease and the HIV antibody (which indicates the presence of AIDS) is becoming necessary in several states.

☐ Some states require physical examinations as well as blood tests.

Bring proper identification.

☐ Driver license, birth certificate, baptismal record, or military service identification can be used as proof of identification.

If you're considered under age.

☐ Under-age persons must have the consent of their parents before obtaining a marriage license.

Divorce or annulment.

☐ If you've been married before, know the date, and place of annulment, and by whom you were divorced. Some states require proof of divorce.

Citizenship.

☐ Those who were born outside the United States will need

identification. Call to ask what identification and papers are needed.

Once you've started the procedure.

☐ A small fee will be requested to pay for the license. The amount varies. In most cases, you'll be able to wait at the office or nearby for an hour or so, for the license to be processed.

Signing the marriage certificate.

☐ Usually the marriage certificate is signed before or after the ceremony.

Witnesses.

☐ Witnesses are usually required. The best man and honor attendant can fulfill these duties.

Marriage certificate ceremony.

☐ Whether or not witnesses are required, some couples include the signing of their marriage certificate in the ceremony or make a separate, special occasion of the signing.

15.
Out-of-Town
Guests

Out-of-town guests need extra planning.

☐ See that comfortable accommodations are available.

☐ Plan for transportation needs of your guests from the time of arrival until their departure.

☐ Develop a list of entertaining activities for them.

Weekend wedding schedule.

☐ Develop a schedule of pre-wedding, wedding, and after-wedding activities. Tuck this into the invitation envelope.

Information package.

☑ Put together a complete information package listing accommodations, transportation, activities, along with exact prices, making clear what the guest is expected to pay. Mail this package at the same time the invitations are sent.

Travel schedule.

☐ Offer the best way to travel to your city, along with at least one alternative. Provide schedules and ticket costs.

Accommodation information.

☐ Give the accommodation information and include the extras that go with it, such as swimming pool, golf course, jogging trail, and complimentary breakfast. Detail the cost so the prices are clear to the guests.

Transportation services.

☐ Offer transportation services from the airport, train, or bus station to your guests' accommodations.

Appropriate attire.

☐ Describe the expected weather conditions and activity schedule and suggest the proper attire.

Contact person.

☐ Be sure to give the name and telephone of a person the

guest can contact in case of last-minute changes or emergencies.

Accommodation reservation deadline.

☐ Emphasize the deadline for making reservations for reserved rooms at the selected hotel.

Transport large groups.

☐ When a large group arrives at the same time, rent a school bus, tour bus, or van. Create a festive atmosphere with Welcome signs on the sides of the vehicles.

Transport small groups.

☐ Smaller groups can be transported by limousines, taxis, or private cars.

Reserving rooms for your guests.

☐ Reserve a block of rooms at one hotel so guests can mingle with each other. You may get a price break for renting several rooms together.

☐ If you do rent a block of rooms—thirty, for instance—ask the management if you are responsible for all thirty rooms or if there is a release date. The release date is the date by which your guests must reserve a room; after that, the rooms that have not been reserved by your guests can be rented by the hotel to other guests.

Send the information to your guests.

☐ A good idea is to include with the invitation, a printed slip of paper saying a block of rooms has been reserved at *(name of hotel)* at *(the rate of)*. Please call *(phone number of hotel)* before *(cutoff date)*.

Cutoff date.

☐ Find out if guests are still eligible for the special rate after the cutoff date.

Friends or relatives as hosts.

☐ In some cases, you may wish to ask close friends or relatives to host special out-of-town guests.

Hospitality room.

☐ Ask the hotel to set up a hospitality room for guests to mingle with one another after arriving.

Meeting place.

☐ Prearrange a meeting place for everyone after they've arrived at their accommodations.

Hospitality hour.

☐ Host a hospitality hour at your home to brief everyone on the festivities in store for them.

Dinner for guests.

☐ Plan a relaxed dinner at a favorite restaurant or a helpful relative or friend's house.

Wedding morning breakfast.

☐ Invite everyone to a morning breakfast buffet the day of the wedding.

Send-off-the-couple party.

☐ Plan a send-off-the-couple party the day after the wedding. Make it casual to contrast with the fancy doings of the day before.

When you can't personally entertain.

☐ Arrange a guided tour of the city or area.
☐ Make group reservations so everyone can meet and dine at a good restaurant.
☐ Provide deli lunch bags and transportation for a picnic in a park or beach area.
☐ Supply tickets to a local sports event.

Schedule free time for your guests.

☐ Perhaps the best time to schedule free time is the morning of the wedding. Guests may want a leisurely time to wake up and get ready for the wedding.

Free time to shop.

☐ Some may appreciate free time to visit your list of recommended shops. Provide information about transportation to good shopping areas.

Plan activities for guests' free time.

☐ List points of interest you know your guests will enjoy—for instance, a walk along a beach or in an area of architectural interest.

☐ Suggest activities such as biking, jogging, or working out and include rental, trail, and where-to-find information.

Give your guests a special welcome.

☑ Welcome your guests with a fruit basket or a bottle of wine with cheese and crackers.

☐ Surprise everyone with tickets to a play, sporting event, or family entertainment center.

☑ Supply newspapers, magazines, and any other appropriate reading material.

☐ Announce the beginning of this special time with T-shirts waiting for them declaring, "I'm a special guest!"

☐ Don't forget about a good, old-fashioned hug and a sincere smile of welcome.

Prepare the final schedule of events.

☐ Any schedule will look more appealing if a little creativity is used in its presentation. Print the schedule on good-quality paper. Use calligraphy or fine handwriting—just make sure everything is readable. You may want to go so far as to draw a border or motif on the schedule that mirrors the wedding theme. Be sure everyone receives a schedule.

Supply a mini-directory.

☐ Out-of-town guests will appreciate having a list of other guests with the telephone numbers of where they can be reached.

Appoint a representative.

☐ Since you are going to be busy with other things, ask a friend or relative to see that the out-of-town guests are taken care of. Give your guests the name and telephone number of your substitute so they have someone to contact in case of questions.

Find reliable babysitters.

☐ If there will be small children, find a babysitter who can take care of the children when the parents are busy elsewhere. Give the babysitter's telephone number and the hourly charge to the guests, and let them make their own arrangements.

Put together a care package.

☐ Guests will appreciate maps to the city, bus, or subway schedules, a list of car rentals, suggested restaurants, and a list of events. You might go so far as to include packets of aspirin, lotion, and if appropriate, sunscreen.

16.
Children

Children as guests.

☐ Infants and children under 5 present a special dilemma at weddings. Children 5 or older should be able to attend the ceremony quietly and eat and behave well at the reception.

An adults-only wedding.

☐ The question of children is answered if both sides of the family agree on an adults-only invitation list. Simply word the invitations in a way that lets your guests know that children are not invited.

Family customs.

☐ When one or both families are accustomed to bringing children to weddings, then accommodations for children must be planned.

Child care during the ceremony.

☑ Use the wedding site nursery, or if it doesn't have a nursery, use an empty, childproof room near a bathroom. Hire older teenagers to babysit.

☐ Instruct the ushers and greeters to direct the parents to the nursery.

☐ Should the church or synagogue not have an area you can use, set up a temporary nursery in the home of a nearby relative.

Child care during the reception.

☑ Most parents will be relieved if you set up a nursery where children under 5 can play and have something to eat.

☐ If your reception is at a hotel, you may already have arranged blocks of rooms for out-of-town guests. Use one of these rooms as a nursery.

☐ If you haven't reserved rooms, perhaps the hotel management will throw in an extra room with the reception package. Make sure the room is safe for children and near a bathroom.

Let your guests know about available babysitters.

☐ Insert a formally printed card in the invitation that says a nursery and babysitter will be available for children under 5 during the ceremony and reception.

☐ If the nursery has to be separate from the ceremony or reception site, draw maps to the nursery and send them with the enclosure cards.

Involve the children of guests in the wedding activities.

☐ Invite the older children to assist the cake cutter, watch the gift table, or hand out favors to your guests.

☐ Hand them an inexpensive camera and instruct them to take pictures throughout the wedding day.

☐ Ask one of the children to collect keepsakes of the wedding for your collection and for theirs.

☐ Any child will be honored to have a special picture taken with the bride and groom and thrilled when they receive the picture after the wedding.

☐ If you're having a theme wedding, perhaps the children could dress in costume to represent your theme. For example, they could dress as pages at a medieval theme wedding.

☐ Two or three of the children could emphasize your heritage by dressing up in ethnic costumes.

Children in the wedding party.

☐ Children under five in a wedding party is risky. Children over five can usually understand what is expected of them.

Ring bearer.

☐ The ring bearer, usually 5 to 8 years old, carries only costume-jewelry wedding rings on the pillow in the wedding procession. The real rings are with the honor attendant.

Flower girl.

☐ The flower girl, usually 5 to 8 years old, carries a cluster bouquet, a small basket of flowers, or a basket of flower petals which she sprinkles on the aisle.

Pages.

☐ Pages are young children who follow the bride, holding the end of her train. They may be boys or girls.

Junior bridesmaid.

☐ Junior bridesmaids are between 9 and 14 years old. They precede the bridesmaids in the processional. Usually they don't have an escort.

Children from a previous marriage.

☐ Invite your children to be members of your wedding party. Be aware, though, that children under 18 can't be legal witnesses to your marriage.

☐ Teenage children can be junior bridesmaids or ushers. Younger children will enjoy the role of ring bearer and flower girl.

Other ways to include your children in the ceremony.

☐ Your children can act as greeters at the entrance to the ceremony, pass out programs, or present single, stemmed flowers to the guests.

☐ Ushers can escort your children to special seats just before the processional begins.

☐ Children will feel included if they are mentioned in a prayer or in a special sentiment written into the ceremony.

Include your children at the reception.

☐ Give your children things to do at the reception. Ask them to be in charge of the guest book or punch bowl, or ask them to make a toast at the dinner table.

☐ Make sure your children are included in the wedding photographs.

☐ If there is a dance, include them after the bride and groom's dance.

Before the wedding.

☐ Beforehand, remember to ask your children's opinions about as many wedding decisions as you or they can handle.

17.
Pre-Wedding Parties

Announce your engagement to close family members.

☐ Plan an intimate buffet dinner for close family members. Choose a select moment during the course of the evening to announce your engagement.

Formally announcing your engagement.

☐ Invite family and friends to a private dinner dance. At an appropriate time and with a flourish from the band, a parent or old friend formally announces your engagement.

Announce your engagement at a casual get-together.

☐ Plan a casual day at the cabin or weekend home with friends and relatives. At a moment when everyone is gathered together, announce your engagement to the group.

Plan an engagement party.

☐ Rent a jukebox or hire a disc jockey and invite everyone to your engagement party. Let the good times roll in celebration of your engagement.

A holiday announcement.

☐ A holiday gathering is a good opportunity to announce your engagement. Everyone is there already and in a festive mood. Your announcement will simply add to the joy and gaity.

It's really a fitting party.

☐ Enjoy this day of final fitting and shoe selection topped with a festive lunch, at home or at a good restaurant. Take this opportunity to give your bridesmaids their thank-you gifts.

Inviting made easy.

☐ Invite your friends to an invitation work party. Consider it part work, part conversation, and part good eating. Only the best handwriters or calligraphy artists address the envelopes . . . the rest stuff envelopes, lick seals, and stamp.

Sampling tastes.

☐ Let your testing panel—the wedding party or a few good friends—sample two or three wedding cakes and icings, as well as two or three varieties of chilled champagne. Color code each sample and ask your guests for their favorites.

Assemble-a-favor party.

☐ Employ an assembly line of friends to help make and package the wedding favors. Treat the workers to pizza and beverages after the work is through.

Decking the hall.

☐ Whisk in and out of the reception site with a bevy of workers, decorating props in hand, on the morning of the wedding. Coffee, juice, and breakfast rolls should give your workers needed energy and an excuse for turning decorating time into a mini pre-wedding celebration.

A moving celebration.

☐ Moving your possessions to a new home can be as fun as a party. Pack everything in advance. The day of the move, organize your helpers so some are putting the boxes and furniture on a rental truck or van and some are waiting to unpack. Be ready with beer, pop, pizza, and a selection of fast, rhythmic music to make the job go faster and seem easier.

For the bride and groom shower.

☐ Join the trend toward couples showers. Plan activities and a menu that include everyone. Good beginnings are guaranteed.

Showers can be more than kitchen and bath stuff.

☐ Use imagination for the shower theme. Turn to hardware, fix-it, and special-interest categories for more varied and interesting gift selections. Everyone needs things like a hammer, glue, and flashlight when setting up a new home.

Family-style shower.

☐ The whole family can take part in the shower. Children love these family occasions and the adults will get a chance to meet the rich relative from the "other" side of the family.

Women-only shower.

☐ This elegant shower starts with a museum tour and winds up with a lovely luncheon. The guests, as well as the bride, will appreciate the quality time.

The do-something shower.

☐ Showers need not be only gifts, food, and chatter. Think of activities to keep everyone entertained. Plan wine and cheese tastings, learn-something-new demonstrations, or active pool or beachside games.

Bridesmaids' luncheon.

☑ You and your bridesmaids should enjoy an intimate time together, a kind of time-out occasion. A luncheon, either at home or in a quiet restaurant, can lend a festive spirit to this time of togetherness. This is a good time to give your presents to the bridesmaids.

Bridesmaids' teatime.

☐ Set aside a time in the afternoon for a pretty, nostalgic

tea with your bridesmaids. Create a Victorian setting with lace tablecloth, floral china, and a scone and biscuit menu. Enjoy a slow, drifting afternoon before you go back to your list of things to do.

Bridesmaids' tanning treat.

☐ Treat your bridesmaids to a visit to the suntanning spa. Munch on light refreshments and let everyone have an opportunity to spend time under the tanning lights.

Bridesmaid make-over tips.

☐ Plan a get-together with your bridesmaids and invite a makeup expert to the party. Bring swatches of the dresses so just-right makeup can be planned for the wedding day.

Laugh time for the bridesmaids.

☐ Plan a night out at a comedy club. Enjoy the goodwill and congeniality with your bridesmaids that only a night of laughs can produce.

Dance the night away.

☐ Take the bridesmaids to everyone's favorite dancing den and dance the night away. There's nothing like rhythmic dance to chase those wedding-planning tensions away.

Groom's card night.

☐ Turn an apartment living room into a gaming room and feature one-eyed jacks as the main attraction of the night. Add the groom's attendants and plenty of refreshments.

Groom's sporting event.

☐ A sporting event is just the ticket for a pre-wedding night out for the groom and his attendants. A dinner beforehand isn't necessary, but it does round out the evening nicely.

Groom's day at the racetrack.

☐ Bring the party to the racetrack and place your winning

bets. With any luck, everyone will come away with a few extra dollars in their pockets.

A bicycle marathon for the groom's party.

☐ Join a bicycle marathon to get everyone in shape for the wedding day. After the ride, give the attendants and ushers a thank-you gift, perhaps a bicycle accessory.

Groom's camping weekend.

☐ Enjoy a leisurely weekend of camping and canoeing. This men-only party should be filled with a spirit of camaraderie and just plain fun.

At-home rehearsal dinner.

☐ Invite the wedding party members and close family members to an intimate dinner at your home. Plan cocktails and sit-down buffet dinner to relax everyone before the big day.

A Camelot-theme rehearsal dinner.

☐ Reserve a room or tables at a restaurant with English tudor decor. Roll out the red carpet for the royal couple and their attendants. Entertain the court after dinner with a strolling lute player and a juggling show.

Highlight the groom's sport interest.

☐ One parent took his son's interest in hockey and built the rehearsal dinner theme around ice and hockey sticks. The evening started with a school bus collecting the guests and taking them to an ice arena, where the dinner was catered.

The common-interest rehearsal dinner.

☐ Should the groom and bride have a common interest such as music or the same profession, tie their interest to the rehearsal dinner theme. Keep this interest in mind when choosing the table appointments, menu, or party favors.

Countrify the rehearsal dinner.

☐ Bring the rehearsal dinner to the country and enjoy a country-style menu. Listen to fiddle, guitar, or accordian music, and dance the Virginia reel, the two-step, or square dance.

The ethnic or regional-flavored rehearsal dinner.

☐ Now is the time to accentuate the positives of one's ethnic or regional background. Dramatic costumes, authentic recipes, and special family customs will double the enjoyment and delight of the party.

The wedding-morning breakfast.

☐ Guests from out of town will especially appreciate a wake-up breakfast of juice, pancakes, and maple syrup. Perhaps your aunt could host this event instead of a shower.

The day-after picnic.

☐ An informal backyard picnic the day after the wedding is just the right contrast to the formal wedding. Have the picnic catered, or ask the guests to bring their best potluck dishes.

The wedding weekend roast-and-toast.

☐ This good natured get-together of the wedding guests features a roast-and-toast of the wedding couple. Sneak in a family slide show, too. It's all in good fun.

Include a special family occasion in the wedding weekend.

☐ A weekend of wedding festivities will be doubly blessed by taking time to mark the occasion of your parents' wedding aniversary or a grandmother's birthday. It's one more excuse for everyone to get together and celebrate.

The wedding weekend sightseeing tour.

☐ Pack all the out-of-town guests into a van or tour bus and show them the area's points of interest. Pack deli lunch bags on board for everyone

The wedding wind-down party.

☐ Let everyone wind down at a relaxed, late-night pool setting. Use a private pool or the pool facilities of your out-of-town guests' hotel.

Simultaneous wedding parties.

☐ Sometimes planning one kind of party just isn't enough to hold the interests of all your weekend guests. Plan several types of activities for the same time and let your guests choose for themselves. For example, schedule an inner tube float down a nearby river, a croquet and lawn party, and an excursion to a local sporting event, all at the same time.

After-the-wedding hometown introduction.

☐ When one spouse is from another city, a hometown gala is in order. Invite everyone to a good restaurant or country club for dinner, dancing, and the opportunity to meet the wedding couple.

Meet-the-relatives barbecue.

☐ Put on a backyard barbecue for those relatives who couldn't make the wedding. This is their chance to share the joy of the new couple.

Moving to your spouse's city.

☐ This is an opportunity for the friends of your spouse to introduce themselves and their homes with a progressive dinner party. Each family hosts a different part of the meal in their home.

A surprise announcement.

☐ Those couples who have married quietly can still bask in their friends' and relatives' good wishes. Simply invite everyone to a party and then announce the marriage. This solves the problem of asking guests not to bring gifts, as well.

18.
Wedding
Gifts

Using a gift registry.

☐ Registering at a gift registry service makes sense for you and your guests. It will help guests to choose gifts that reflect your tastes and needs.

What is a gift registry?

☐ A gift registry is a free service offered by your local department or gift store giving you the opportunity to list the things you need. In turn, your guests have the opportunity to look over your list and choose an appropriate gift.

Before you register.

☐ Take some time to think about and discuss your combined tastes in housekeeping and design. Be sure both of you take part in this step.

Making an appointment.

☐ Call for an appointment ahead of time so you're sure you'll have all the help and time you need to make your decisions.

When should you register?

☐ You should register soon after you announce your wedding date. Give the name of the store to your friends and family so they can use this service for shower gifts as well as the wedding gifts.

Where can you register?

☐ Most couples register at a department store, gift store, or jewelry and tableware store.

☐ Other places to register are hardware stores, special-interest stores, such as camping or bicycling supply stores, and gourmet stores.

Gift giving before the wedding.

☐ Some gifts will be sent to your home a few weeks before the wedding. Be sure your home address (where you are living before the wedding) is listed on the gift registry.

Gifts at the wedding.

☐ Since gifts will be brought to the reception, you should have a display table ready and someone appointed to look after the gifts.

Gifts sent after the wedding.

☐ Since it is socially correct to send gifts after the wedding, you can expect gifts up to a year, but generally only about one month, after the wedding. Be sure your new home address is available.

Displaying gifts.

☐ Set up a table in your home to display the gifts. Unwrap each gift, tape the name to the box or underneath the gift item, and record the information in your filing system.

Naming the gift giver.

☐ It's not in the best taste to display the name of the gift giver with the gift. Gift giving is not a competition.

Bringing gifts to the reception.

☐ Don't bring gifts from your home to display at your reception.

Decorating the gift display table.

☐ Cover the display table with a white tablecloth. Curl ribbons the length of the table and attach bows or poseys to the corners and edges of the table.

Gift security.

☐ Ask a relative or close friend to keep an eye on the gifts. Safeguard against accidental breakage or disappearance of the gifts.

Bringing gifts home from the reception.

☐ Arrange with your parents, attendants, or close friends to take the gifts for safekeeping after the wedding celebration.

Gifts received at the reception.

☐ It's not a good idea to open gifts brought to the reception because it takes time that should be spent mingling with your guests.

The formal gift opening.

☐ It is the trend in most areas today to extend the wedding celebration with the day-after gift-opening party. In this case, only close family, friends, and attendants attend.

Thank-you remarks.

☐ Try to moderate your remarks when opening the gifts so that everyone is sincerely thanked and no one is embarrassed by too much or too little gratitude.

How to say thank you when money is given.

☐ Whenever a gift of money is received, don't mention the amount, but say something like "Thank you for the generous gift." When you write your thank-you note, mention how you will be using the money.

☐ Display the gift card, but put the check or cash in the bank.

Receiving similar gifts.

☐ Try not to comment on the similarity of gifts. Simply give a sincere thank you. After the wedding festivities, quietly exchange one of the gifts. If you don't know where the gift was purchased, try to inquire discreetly.

Displaying similar gifts.

☐ Similar gifts should not be displayed together; place them in separate areas. If they are absolute doubles, simply display just one of them.

Broken or damaged gifts.

☐ Quietly call the store where the gift was purchased and tell them the condition in which the gift arrived. Most stores will see to it that a duplicate gift is sent without the gift giver being told.

Protect your gifts.

☐ Leave gifts with your family or a good friend while you are away on your honeymoon.

☐ Ask a friend to house sit for you until you return.

☐ Let the neighbors know when you're going to leave and when to expect you back.

☐ It may be worthwhile to get a supplement to your household insurance policy, especially if you have received many valuable gifts.

What to say about a "What is it?" type of gift.

☐ Do your best when you receive a gift and you can't figure out what it is. If this happens when you are opening gifts in front of an audience, perhaps your mother or an older friend can come to your rescue. Plan for this kind of help ahead of time. Otherwise, just say a simple thank you.

Gifting the attendants.

☐ Give each attendant a gift chosen to match their personal interest or activity.

☐ Engrave gifts with the attendants' initials and the date of the wedding.

☐ Use your wedding theme for gift inspiration. For example, a Victorian theme could inspire you to give ornate silver picture frames. (For more wedding themes, see *Wedding Plans: 50 Unique Themes for the Wedding of Your Dreams*. Write to Brighton Publications, Inc., P.O. Box 12706, New Brighton, MN 55112 for ordering information.)

Gift ideas for bridesmaids.

☐ Look for monogrammed handkerchiefs, lace gloves, perfume bottles, decorative hair combs, potpourri hearts, charm bracelets, tickets to the ballet, a pretty parasol, or silk flowers.

Gift ideas for the groom's attendants.

☐ The male attendants will enjoy cuff links, leather gloves, a money clip, stein, silk handkerchief, neck scarf, theater tickets, miniature classic car model, or pocket knife.

Gift ideas for everyone.

☐ All the attendants can use fountain pens with ink, picture frames, candleholders, glass sun catcher, gift package of candy, fruit, and nuts, a bottle of wine or champagne, address book, letter opener, hand-blown goblet, or pewter mug.

Thank your parents.

☐ Weddings are an especially good time to say thank you for everything your parents have done for you through the years. Whether it's a personal note, a bouquet of flowers, candy, or a balloon that says "Super Parents," give your parents something that says, "I love you."

Give your wedding helpers a thank you.

☐ Remember, any of your friends or relatives who contributed to your wedding should receive a token gift and a thank-you note. This includes the soloist, the friend who styled your hair, the aunt who served the cake, or the nephews who passed out single, stemmed flowers at the ceremony.

"Help!"
Hints
19.

Split seams or missing buttons.

☐ Bring a travel sewing kit that includes thread, buttons, needles, and scissors for small sewing emergencies.

No time for stitching.

☐ Safety pins are good for last-minute fixes. They can hold zippers together and tuck up dragging hem lines.

Hosiery snags.

☐ Use clear nail polish to catch snags and runs in nylon stockings before they become major disasters.

Stains from wine and other beverages.

☐ Sponge the wine stain with a cloth dampened in club soda.

Car door stains and other greasy stuff.

☐ Prepare for greasy stains by bringing a small container of cleaning solvent or spray-on spot remover. Place the stain face down on a paper towel and blot the back of the stain from center to edge. Add a little soap and water and blot dry.

Cover a hard-to-remove stain on the bridal dress.

☐ Sprinkle talcum powder on the spot to hide the stain until after the wedding when the dress can be dry cleaned.

Protect the edge of long dresses.

☐ Spray the hem and any part of the bridal dress train that may touch the ground with a fabric protector like Scotchguard before the wedding. Always check the instructions first.

Boutonniere pin pricks.

☐ When an overzealous helper jabs the usher with a boutonniere pin, apply an adhesive bandage quickly to the spot. If you're too late and blood stains his white shirt, dab on a little club soda to dilute the blood. Otherwise, tell the usher to keep his jacket closed.

Lost cuff links or earrings.

☐ Better safe than sorry. Bring along extras just in case. In a pinch, safety pins can take the place of the cuff links.

Cosmetic and hair fix-ups.

☐ Bring along a bag containing extra cosmetics, nail polish, hair spray, combs, brushes, mirrors, and curling iron.

Extra personal protection.

☐ Bring extra deodorant spray, dental floss, and any needed personal hygiene pads.

Sore feet or broken heels.

☐ An extra pair of shoes is a welcome relief when your feet are protesting high-fashion shoes. The extra pair comes in handy, too, in case a heel breaks off during an enthusiastic wedding dance.

Shoe mix-up.

☐ If the bride wears two pairs of shoes, one pair for beauty and one pair for comfort, make sure the pretty pair is always worn at the right time, for example, at photo-taking time.

Wrinkle free.

☐ Look for wrinkle-free aerosal spray in the notions department. It's great to smooth out those wrinkles that appear from sitting.

Clinging problems.

☐ An aerosol spray will prevent clothes from clinging. This can be a real problem during the dry, winter months. Look in the notions section of a department store or the grocery store.

Wine stains on the table linen.

□ Sprinkle the stain with table salt. Brush off when dry. Later rub the stain out in cold water before washing.

Cracks in the wedding cake.

□ Cover accidental cracks in the cake with fresh flower blossoms, green leaves, or decorative candies.

Help from the kitchen.

□ Sometimes a cake can be repaired with help from the kitchen staff or caterer. They may have icing bags that can be filled with frosting or whipped cream to repair the damage decoratively.

Personal delivery.

□ The last thing the bride should do is attempt to bring the cake to the reception herself. With so much on her mind, she is likely to do something terrible—like drop the cake on the floor.

Plenty of cameras, but no film.

□ Remember to pack extra film in the camera bag. A few extra cameras to pass out to willing guests will help you catch those precious candid shots.

Group pictures.

□ Watch out for group photos. If you don't want to look like a size 46, forget about stretching your arms around the person next to you. Your dress, especially around the arm area, will expand and make you look as big as a blimp.

Tired children.

□ Make arrangements with an older teenager to take tired children to an adjacent room for a little quiet time. Bring storybooks and sleeping mats or bags just in case the little ones might need some shut-eye.

Seating opportunities.

☐ The older folk, as well as other guests, will appreciate chairs conveniently placed so they can sit down occasionally. Make sure some seating is available near the receiving line.

Candle checkups.

☐ Check the ceremony candles and unity candle, especially if the candles were lighted for the photography session. Clean off any wax buildup around the wick area so the candles will burn evenly during the ceremony.

Fire hazard.

☐ Wearing net head pieces or a bridal veil is part of the wedding tradition. But you do have to be careful not to stand too close to a burning candle. It takes just a second to set the netting on fire.

20.
Thank-You Notes

Making time for the thank yous.

☐ Believe it or not, you can find time for writing your notes of thanks. Use time immediately after opening the gift at home, evenings after work, or a weekend after the honeymoon. Snatch moments whenever you can—as you ride to work, while you wait in the doctor's office, or any other little snippets of free time.

Help is your nearest companion.

☐ Since your husband is the beneficiary of these beautiful wedding gifts as well, give him the opportunity to say thanks to his relatives, friends, and co-workers.

Organization is the key word.

☐ As soon as the gift is opened, put the gift card inside the box or tape it on the gift. Add any information to the card that will help you identify the gift if the card should fall off.

☐ If you have a card file of invited guests, put the gift information on the card. Then you'll have the name, address, and gift information in one place.

Choosing the appropriate stationery.

☐ Informal cards with *Thank You* printed on them are the most common choice for weddings today.

☐ Formal weddings demand a 4 x 5-inch card that matches your wedding stationary. You may use your name only, your spouse's name only (if he is writing thank yous), or both your names together. Most couples prefer a monogram.

Adding a photograph to the thank-you note.

☐ An extra touch for thank-you notes is the inclusion of a photograph of you as a couple and the gift giver or a formal photograph of you and your spouse. Some stationers have thank-you notes that have slots in the front to hold the photograph.

Preprinted thank-you cards.

☐ Sorry, but using a thank-you card with a commercial message thanking the gift giver is going to make you look either silly or lazy. There is no good excuse invented yet to use this kind of note. Thus far, these notes are truly not acceptable.

Who deserves a thank you?

☐ Anyone who sent a gift or provided a personal service for your wedding deserves a thank you. Some examples of those who you may want to thank are the soloist, the cake cutter, and the babysitter for the guests' children.

Necessary information for writing thank-you notes.

☐ The three most important pieces of information you should have at hand are the name (both names if it is a couple), address, and the gift given.

The opening sentence.

☐ The first thing the reader of the note should know is who is saying thank you. You can make things easier on yourself if you first make a key list of possible phrases to begin the opening sentence. These phrases can be as simple as "Allen and I are so pleased . . . ," "I would like to thank you . . . ," or "We were so excited . . . ," Then consult this list to help you get started writing your thank-you note.

If you can't say something nice . . .

☐ Your next step is to say something nice about the gift. Here again, you can use the list trick. Find descriptive, but appropriate, words for your list. Words such as *beautiful, interesting, eye-catching, sentimental,* and *thoughtful* are always good, but try to find more words that best fit the gift. A dictionary can help you. Make this list as long as you can so you don't have to stop and search for a word in the middle of writing your thank-you notes.

Where or how the gift will be used.

☐ The gift giver always appreciates knowing where or how the gift will be used. So at the same time you are talking glowingly about the gift, mention a time when you will use the gift. Some things you might say are "The linens add the perfect color to our bedroom," or "The silver tray is the center attraction in our dining room."

Add a personal thought to your note.

☐ In most cases you'll be able to add a personal comment. Of course, it depends on the person you are thanking, but some things you could add are "It was so nice to meet you at the wedding. John has always had such nice things to say about you," or "We can't wait to use the silver when we have you for our first at-home dinner party guests," or "Mom and Dad always told me how kind you were and now we know firsthand."

Before you conclude.

☐ Thank the gift giver again at the end of your note. It can be something as simple as "Thank you so much," "Many thanks," or "Please accept our thank you again." The closing sentence should be in the same spirit as what you have already said.

The ending.

☐ Your sign-off should be appropriate to the person who is receiving the note. A warm "Love always" or "Much affection" sent to family or close friends is always welcomed. For acquaintances or business associates, a "Sincerely" or "Yours" is better. For those in between, you can say "Cordially," "Your friends." and "Best regards."

Your signature.

☐ Use your maiden name if you are writing and sending thank-you notes before the wedding.

☐ Sign your new name, if you are using your husband's name, after the wedding.

☐ It's also acceptable to use both your husband's name and your name together. This can mean your full name and your spouses, or it can be the more traditional "Mr. and Mrs."

The return address.

☐ Use the address you are using before the wedding when sending notes. After the marriage, of course, use your new at-home address.

Keep a record.

☐ Whatever system you have, be sure to reserve a place to jot down the date you sent the thank-you card. For one thing, writing it down will act as a psychological reward and it will help you prove to your mother that you did indeed send a thank you to Aunt Sue.

Timing can be important.

☐ Sending a thank-you note in reasonable time to the gift giver shows you care that they took the time to select and purchase a gift. Before the wedding, send out a thank you after each gift arrives. After the wedding and honeymoon, try to get the notes out at least within four to six weeks.

Thank yous before and after the wedding.

☐ Before the wedding, it makes sense to mail the notes in dribs and drabs. But after the wedding, it is probably better to send all the notes at once. This will prevent Cousin Mary from calling and asking why she didn't receive a thank-you note when Aunt Ellen received her note.

"Received the Gift" notes.

☐ Some wedding couples order printed "Received the Gift" notes at the same time they order their wedding stationary. They do this when they know they can't get their personal thank-you notes in the mail within four to six weeks after the wedding. The note acknowledges receipt of the gift and tells the sender that a personal thank-you note will follow. See what your stationer has to offer.

When wedding plans are interrupted.

☐ When a wedding is cancelled, any gifts received should be returned with a short note of explanation and a thank you. You send the notes and gifts to your friends and family, and the groom-to-be will assume the responsibility for his friends and family. Decide who will be responsible for your shared friends.

Newspaper announcements.

☐ About two weeks before the wedding, send the full names of you, your groom, and both sets of parents. Give the wedding date, time, and place information. If you wish, you can add your honeymoon destination and your new at-home address. Giving address information can be a security risk, so consider this carefully. Include a black-and-white photograph.

☐ Since some newspapers have forms to follow, you will only have to give specific facts, spell accurately, and observe deadlines.

☐ Ordinarily, your community newspaper will devote more space to your wedding than will a newspaper for a large metropolitan area.

☐ If one or both have strong ties to another city, send the announcements to the out-of-town newspaper, as well.

The Honeymoon
21.

When to plan for the honeymoon.

☐ Start making plans for your honeymoon as soon as you decide on the wedding date. If your wedding is to take place around Valentine's Day, the peak travel season, you should start making plans at least six months ahead of time.

Budgeting for the honeymoon.

☐ It's a good idea to budget the honeymoon expenses at the same time as the wedding day plans. Discuss how much both of you want to spend on your holiday and try to match your dreams to the budget.

Looking for travel help.

☐ Ask your friends and relatives to recommend a travel agent. Most likely, if they were satisfied, you will be too.

☐ Look in the travel sections of your newspaper and call the agents listed. Keep looking until you find someone you're comfortable with.

Give the travel agent some help.

☐ Have the total travel budget in mind so the agent can keep travel suggestions within your guidelines.

☐ Discuss what you both would enjoy doing. Bring several ideas. The travel agent may be able to find a place to satisfy more than one wish.

☐ To get the best service and most enjoyable trip, plan early. Don't wait until the month before the wedding.

What to expect from the travel agent.

☐ The agent should be able to offer suggestions about the best kinds of holiday for a newly married couple.

☐ Ask for recommendations for the best places to stay and the most reliable transportation.

☐ All paperwork should be taken care of by the agent. This is often a free service because hotels and airlines pay travel agents commissions.

☐ Ask about luggage regulations, arrival and departure times, and any passport or immunization requirements.

Complete honeymoon packages.

☐ Cruises are ideal because everything except transportation is included in the package. Meals and entertainment are already paid for. It's an easy way to manage expenses. You are also pampered with services.

☐ Many hotels and resorts have three-night-four-day, or seven-night-eight-day packages. Each package is different, so make sure you understand all the details.

Additional costs.

☐ Remember that there may be additional costs. Budget for such extras as meals, car rental, admission, and sightseeing tour costs.

Packing for your trip.

☐ Roll each item of clothing before putting it in the suitcase. It will cut down on wrinkles and save space.

☐ Pack each article of clothing in a resealable plastic bag. The trapped air cushions the clothing and cuts down on wrinkling. This method takes up more space in your suitcase, but it does cut down on wrinkling, especially of rayon pieces.

☐ Don't worry about trying to remember the toothpaste, suntan lotion, and so on. These things can always be purchased when you reach your destination.

Safety tips for travel.

☐ Buy traveler's checks. It's a good idea to have traveler's checks in both your names, in case of emergencies.

☐ Keep credit cards and your bank cash card in a secure place. Take any unnecessary credit cards, papers, or treasured pictures out of your billfold or purse before leaving on your trip.

☐ Don't trust the security of your rooms. Check jewelry and cash into the hotel's safe-deposit boxes. Some hotels have a safe-deposit box in each room.

Insurance plans for travelers.

☐ Check into insurance plans available for travelers. Plans such as baggage insurance or trip-cancellation plans may be worth the extra cost.

☐ If you're traveling outside the United States, go over your health insurance plan. Some companies will not cover you when you are traveling outside the United States.

Proper identification.

☐ You will need proper identification to cash the traveler's checks. Since you will be purchasing the checks before the wedding day, the checks will be issued in the name you are using then. Make sure you have identification for the name used on your checks.

Credit cards.

☐ Major credit cards are widely accepted. Consider using these for preplanned expenses such as hotel bills and transportation expenses. That way there won't be any unpleasant surprises when you get the bill a month later.

Minimum cash.

☐ Take as little cash as possible. However, you will need cash for tipping, for buying small items such as postcards, and so on.

Don't forget the camera.

☐ A small, automatic camera is a must for your trip. If you don't have one you could include this item as a special request on your wedding registry list. Picture albums for the honeymoon pictures make good gift suggestions, too.

Bring home mementos of the trip.

☐ Collect seashells, sand from the seaside, pebbles or small rocks, matchbooks, paper napkins inscribed with the name of your hotel, anything that is free for the asking for your memorabilia box.

☐ Purchase inexpensive postcards, T-shirts, or sun visors for take-home souvenirs or gifts.

☐ Purchase your hotel's beach towel with the hotel's logo for your souvenir. It's a clever reminder of your honeymoon and practical too.

Index

Available from Brighton Publications, Inc.

Games for Wedding Shower Fun by Sharon Dlugosch, Florence Nelson

Wedding Plans: 50 Unique Themes for the Wedding of Your Dreams by Sharon Dlugosch

Wedding Hints & Reminders by Sharon Dlugosch

Wedding Occasions: 101 New Party Themes for Wedding Showers, Rehearsal Dinners, Engagement Parties, and More! by Cynthia Lueck Sowden

Dream Weddings Do Come True: How to Plan a Stress-free Wedding by Cynthia Kreuger

Games for Baby Shower Fun by Sharon Dlugosch

Kid-Tastic Birthday Parties: The Complete Party Planner for Today's Kids by Jane Chase

Romantic At-Home Dinners: Sneaky Strategies for Couples with Kids by Nan Booth/Gary Fischler

Reunions for Fun-Loving Families by Nancy Funke Bagley

An Anniversary to Remember: Years One to Seventy-five by Cynthia Lueck Sowden

Folding Table Napkins: A New Look at a Traditional Craft by Sharon Dlugosch

Table Setting Guide by Sharon Dlugosch

Tabletop Vignettes by Sharon Dlugosch

Don't Slurp Your Soup: A Basic Guide to Business Etiquette by Betty Craig

Hit the Ground Running: Communicate Your Way to Success by Cynthia Kreuger

These books are available in selected stores and catalogs. If you're having trouble finding them in your area, send a self-addressed, stamped, business-size envelope and request ordering information from:

Brighton Publications, Inc.
P.O. Box 120706
St. Paul, MN 55112-0706

or call: 1-800-536-BOOK